BARBARA GUEST

REFLEXIONS ON ART

DÜRER IN THE WINDOW

ROOF BOOKS
NEW YORK

Contents

Barbara Guest began writing for *ARTnews* in December 1952. As a poet among artists she saw firsthand the glorious evolution of New York's art world: the flourishing of Abstract Expressionism and the emergence of the New York School of painting. As one of the great innovators of the New American Poetry and as a figure frequently associated with the New York School, Guest examined the arts with a critical eye as well as a creative one. Guest forged a bond between her poetics and the aesthetics of the artists she was surrounded by, not only as an art reviewer, but also as a collaborator.

It was that bond that led me to approach Barbara Guest in the spring of 2000 and request a meeting to discuss her life and work. At the time I was in graduate school at Mills College in Oakland, California, studying poetry and participating in an independent study that explored the connections between language and visual arts. The role of poet as art reviewer and collaborator became my sole focus after reading Guest's reviews in *ARTnews*. Guest, whose work in both genres is renowned, was a natural choice. What began as an informal interview for the purpose of my class evolved into the tribute that is this collection. Richard Tuttle's design of the book and enthusiastic inclusion of his original artwork has been essential to the success and fruition of the project.

Dürer in the Window offers a selection of Guest's work on art written between the 1950's and 2000. It features the early art reviews, collaborations, longer essays and, of course, poetry. Each component highlights her artistic sensibility, subtle and discreet, full of elegance with an exacting eye. Her work demonstrates the ability of one poet to navigate between the realms of two artistic worlds and maintain an active existence in both. *Dürer in the Window* is a showcase of Barbara Guest's writing and a winning example of collaboration itself.

Africa Wayne

Thank you to the following for their help in making this book possible:

Adrian Turner
Angelos Camillos
Joy Wiener
Walburga Krupp
Carolyn Fay
Elizabeth Willis
Hadley Guest
Sir Roy Dexter

And to all the artists who were gracious enough to allow us to include their images.

A special thanks to:
Vanessa Viola and Bill Goldston of Universal Limited Art Editions, ULAE.

Editor: Africa Wayne.
Book Designer: Richard Tuttle.

ISBN: 1-931824-04-5
Library of Congress Catalog Card No.: 2002092928

Roof Books are distributed by
Small Press Distribution
1341 Seventh Avenue
Berkeley, CA. 94710-1403.
Phone orders: 800-869-7553
spdbooks.org

State of the Arts NYSCA

This book is made possible, in part, with public funds from the New York State Council on the Arts, a state agency.

Roof Books
are published by
Segue Foundation
303 East 8th Street
New York, NY 10009
segue.org

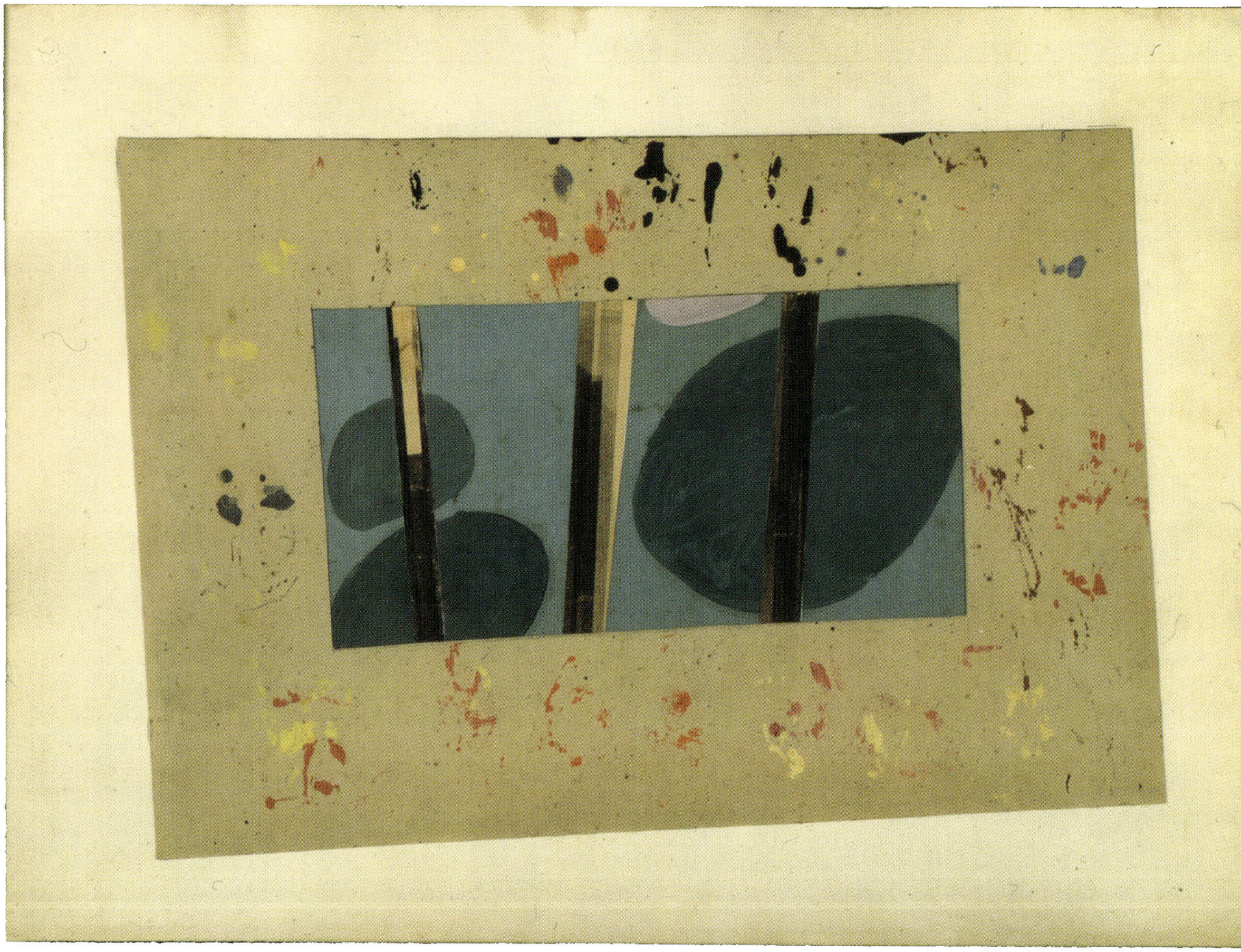

Hans (Jean) Arp, *Dada Collage*, 1918.

JEAN ARP

I like to be in the presence of Arp,
the gentle solace of his anarchy:

> humor
> is water from beyond
> mixed with wine from down here . . .

His first known poems were published in 1903 with the first known drawings on the facing page. He had joined together Art and Poetry and forged there a reality, his life would never permit them to be separated.

His need to simplify structure and then permeate it with pure spatial formality of the cube or oval.

He once showed a friend a sculpture on which there was an almost invisible swelling.

"Do you feel the bump?" he asked.

"I am leaving it as it is. If I get rid of the bump the whole thing will become elegant." This decision relates also to his poetry where we are permitted to read rough passages, and parts of speech. He liked to look up words in the dictionary. He discovered the word, "Eudemonia," which is the "well-being of genius," and it is man's fateful and personal predisposition for happiness, according to Aristotle. This was a discovery for Arp that worked itself into the language of his poetry where "eudemonia" asserts itself.

His poetry contains happiness. You can hear his sculpture:

> "If the guides wear wooden aprons
> the birds wear ankle boots
> the birds are full of echoes
> their eggs roll endlessly from their little hearts
> slowly I climb the milepole
> I put my eggs in the treeholes of the milestones."

Yet his poetry is also filled with *angst.*

Writing about the "inner language," Arp wrote: "The vertical and the horizontal are the extreme signs available to men or touching the beyond and his inwardness." Here he is close to his friend, Kandinsky, who in his book, *Concerning the Spiritual in Art*, wrote of the need for the spiritual in painting that will let artists express their own inner lives in abstract, non-material terms.

When writing of Kandinsky's art, Arp applied the laws of Heraclitus to Kandinsky, who echoes his own belief that, "it is always the same substance that is in all things: life and death, waking and sleeping, youth and old age. For in changing this becomes that, by changing becomes this again."

"Star-in-Boots," written in Alsatian Latin in 1925 was published in the review, *de Stijl*, edited by van Doesburg. It begins and ends on a sound poem interspersed with the fully intelligible lines. It is a collage poem. This poem shows Arp in search of an original universal language that would know neither borders nor nationalities, and would need no translation—only we might acknowledge an inner profound acceptance of the needs of language.

He once said, "a word is fresher to me in French. I know German so very well, ever since school, but French, which I have always spoken, feels like a discovery."

Here we are listening to the two Arps—Hans or Jean—the two first names representing the dual nationalities of Arp who was born in Strasbourg in 1887. His father was from Schleswig-Holstein and his mother was Alsatian. And to further confuse his identity he grew up speaking three languages: French, German, and Alsatian. The latter he learned from his cradle, because it is not a written language, and because it existed in such a loose, such a free style, a word-of-mouth language. He incorporated Alsatian into his early poems, phonetically or in Latinese.

> ...
> naurulam catapult i lem lemn
> haba haba tapam
> his language broke in his mouth
>   (from "Star-in-Boots," 1927)

Arp longed for a communion of artists who would participate in collective works of art and writing in which individual personalities submerged while enriching the whole. This is a Bauhaus concept and today it is as if he had described a lost world of idealism. We must remind ourselves that those combined talents were not lost, or swallowed up, but were the incantation of a group of intensely gifted artists in which the Bauhaus was their collective shrine to the arts.

Arp declared a spiritual dedication to the selflessness which was represented by the Bauhaus and he knew that attitude would enrich art. It is possible that his birth in a "collective place," Alsace, a place where several languages passed on the way to their native tongue, may have contributed to Arp's desire for a collective "one-voiced" art.

Poetry was a continual "work in progress," to Arp, never ended, never completed. Although his poetry appears spontaneous, it went through constant changes and drafts. Even poetry that had been published twenty or thirty years before. Oppositions balance, then contradict one another.

Do you like
the clouds bare
or
covered with plumage?
The night doesn't care about the sky, it saws
the ceiling in half,
the sky doesn't care about the night, it saws the floor
in half.

****

The *Cloud Pumpe* poems were composed around 1911, and were read at Dada evenings where Hugo Ball performed sound poetry in Cubist costume. When tired of political manifestoes, and endless discussions, Dadaists listened to Arp's *Cloud Pumpe* poetry.

The 1924 edition of the *Petit Larousse* defines Dada: "One may consider Dada as the most extreme limit of the possible divorce between words and their meanings."

The *Cloud Pumpe* poems tell how Arp was born in five places.

He was born in the cosmos—a Cloud
in nature
in a pumpe (the mechanical world)
in a skirt (the maternal world)

These poems have a navel which is attached to these worlds—here Arp began his almost obsessive preoccupation with the navel, which appears in both his sculpture and his poetry.

There is a relationship between the poems in *Cloud Pumpe* of 1917, and his relationship between the poems in *papier dechires*, "torn up paper." In these later compositions he "gave free rein to reality and chance." He said that "if you tear up a piece of paper or a drawing, you let in the very essence of life and death."

Arp made many experiments. He was so visual that he declared he saw poems jump from the page! We have a sense always in reading the poems of Arp that they are going to leave us and enter a spatial world where they belong.

He used every "found object," and what he didn't find on the street or in the newspapers, he invented.

He adored senseless jokes, finding in them what he called, "profound reality."

When he settled in Paris in 1925 and met the Surrealists, he began writing directly in French. He mentions this period

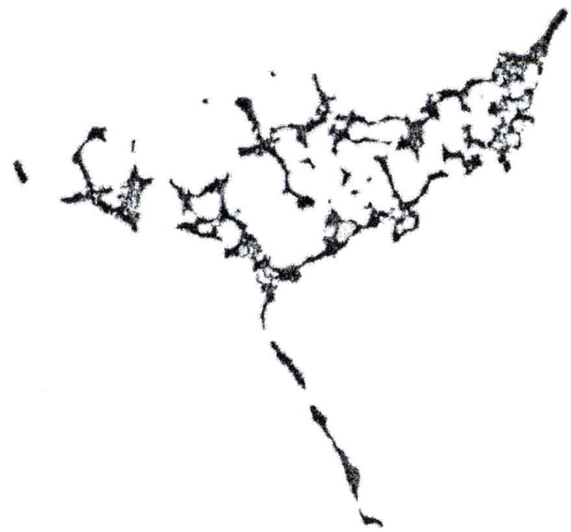

in
a poem: "In those years I
wrote my first poems and my genius
finally manifested itself regardless of my neighbors." His wife, or companion, as he called her, Sophie Taeuber-Arp, is an artist of talent and originality, whom he met in 1915. Arp said, "it was Sophie Taeuber, who through her clear life showed me the right way, the way of beauty."

The influence is found in many places — his sculpture is copied when a sculptor has need of a brief curve in the axis of the work, and despite the usual product of a craft, desires to reach into the modern, many times in commercial manufacture, the short-cut is a glance at the sculpture of Arp, this desire for a geometric brevity. In poetry when there is well hidden, the need for light to finger the open spaces of a poem.

Arp said, if, to suppose the impossible, I had to choose between the visual arts and the poetry of words, if I had to abandon sculpture or poems, I would choose to write Poems. In the most difficult hours of his life he tells us, he turned to poetry.

A year before his death in 1966, he published "The Dream Captain's Logbook," in which he discloses his pessimism about the development of modern man and the modern world.

The dream captain is
at the end of the road.
He wonders who am I?
Where do I come from?

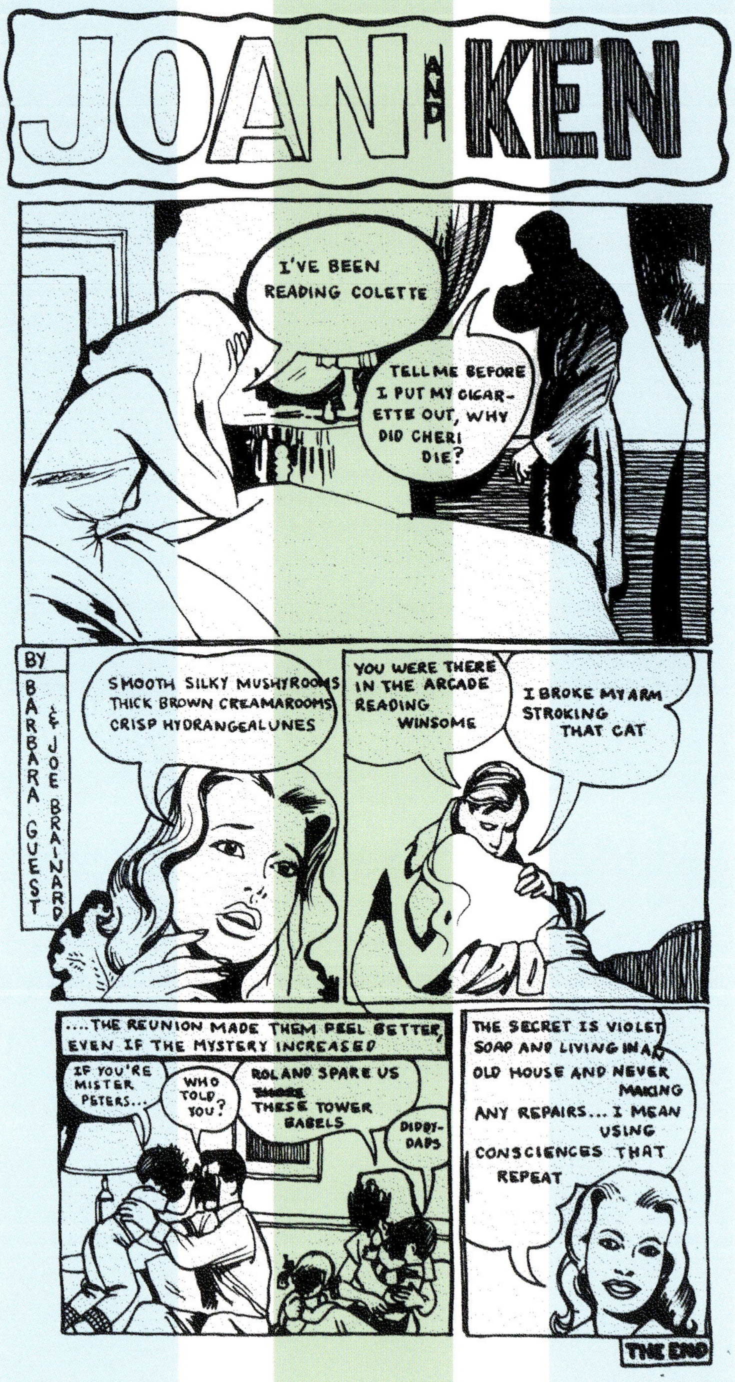

Joe Brainard and Barbara Guest, *Joan and Ken*, ca. 1950.

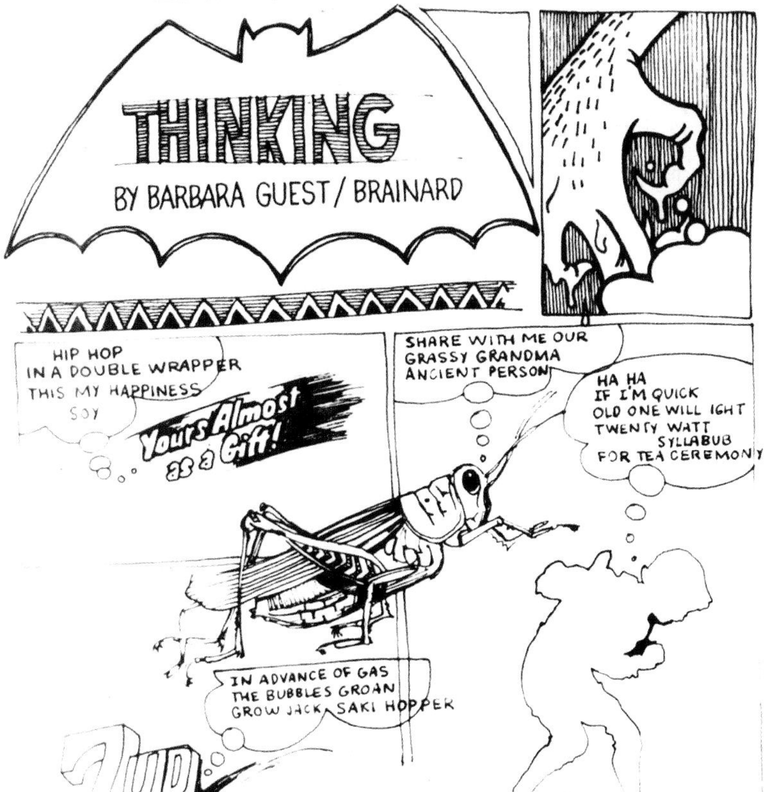

oe Brainard and Barbara Guest, *Thinking*, ca. 1950.

Stephen Etnier [Milch] still exhibits those light, graceful and elegant paintings of the West Indies. And the blue skies and slender natives remain even though he has since moved his locale: many of the present pictures are Maine landscapes, dark, heavy and somber. It is difficult to determine whether or not this is a change for the better. His Maine pictures are more carefully American in tone, almost nineteenth century with their dark greens. At the same time, Etnier handles paint so well that it is highly probable he will later on develop his own genre of New England painting. Nostalgically, for this reviewer, *Shore Road,* a West Indian painting, spacious and lucid, is quite the best of the show.

December 1952

Childe Hassam [Milch] is seen in watercolors (of 1892-1926) which are amazingly fresh and illustrate how closely his paintings and watercolors are aligned. The pictures are all species of Americana, drawn with that particular intent of his to record settings and houses which made up the Eastern seaboard which he knew so well; an intent which in a lesser craftsman might involve mere calligraphy, but in these watercolors revives immediately the tone and color of place which is neither sentimental nor merely topographical. There are the gardens of his friends wherein once again he can allow his Impressionism to run riot with the color of flowers. In *Rocks and Sea*, a drawing which is more completely in his middle style, Impressionism is laid over very thinly and there's a strong imprint of the northern coast of America with its blue which is not quite so cold as one usually expects, but as cold as Hassam could allow it to be. And then there are the regional drawings, such as *General Lee's House, Richmond*, where Hassam is determined that as a sketch-artist he will not allow this one to pass. One also notices in this group, particularly in *September Sky*, an indeterminism, a result of Hassam's recognition that, after all, the style of Impressionism was becoming rather dated, and that he must as a highly egotistical, vigorous artist, and one accustomed to fame, ride the new movements at all costs.

December 1952

Beerbohm and Robinson [American Academy of Arts and Letters] are shown across the court from one another and certainly no more opposing personalities could be collected within a smaller space. Sir Max Beerbohm is represented by caricatures, books, and manuscripts borrowed from private libraries and estates; the organization of this show is pleasantly historical and nostalgic. One realizes, viewing these familiar drawings, the completely unique position Beerbohm occupies within his genre and how undated caricature can become when wisdom and humor dictate its aims. *The Poet's Corner* with "Mr Yeats Introducing George Moore to the Queen of the Fairies," "Byron Shaking the Dust of England from His Toes," or "Tennyson Reading 'In Memoriam' to His Sovereign" are pure and unsucceeded delights. And so are the benign caricature of "Il Pound" and the not so benign caricature of "Mr. Whistler." Passing into an entirely different set of attitudes, Boardman Robinson, the chronicler of the Harding era, begins the long and so far undeveloped reach of American caricature. These drawings are both political newspaper satire and attempts at the portraiture of character. Liberty and mayors, British personalities and war mongering are all rather violently expressed with a pen that now seems a little too sure of itself, a little too romantic, and at the same time willing to go along with the conventional attitudes of the day. The collection itself is excellent and includes several oils.

January 1953

Theodore Stamos' [Parsons] latest paintings continue to move from defined form into the realm of symbol. His paintings in black, ochres, gray and white are nebulous incantations wherein somber forms evoke a series of magic formulas. *Long Island Sounds* has this quality of movement mysteriously hoarded and painted not so much for anyone as for another member of a cult. *Tea House, 7,* has another group of symbols; these are of the East, but still the East as seen by a member of a sect, not a layman or curious traveler, but one of a religious order. As such it is difficult to identify these pictures as they are outwardly constructed quite cohesively, and certainly the tendency of the uninitiated to find in them a kind of decoration may not be relative at all. But there are limitations to be found even within good painting, and here the aura about the pictures has gone too far beyond the ordinary.

January 1953

Richard Stankiewicz [Hansa] is having his first one man show of sculpture composed of aluminum and steel wires covered with white plaster, shredded rope, buttons and bits of tubing. *Fantastic Creatures and Satirical Poses* are witty commentaries on the depravities and demeanors of insect and human life. This group of sculpture is somewhat academic and tight, and several "Poses," like *Tantrum,* remind one of Klee. His latest work is integrated on a much larger scale and moves from direct human experience and observation. *Mounted Man,* of aluminum, wire, screen and plaster, is more brilliant; here he does not attempt to move us emotionally or intellectually, or merely to create a series of intricate designs, but succeeds in drawing us into a spectacle of the human caught in the minor complexities of his minor world. *Problem in Planes* clears out a good deal of unnecessary formula and is merely wire screen balanced on three levels. This small sculpture should mark the beginning of development toward a pure and personal style on a high level.

January 1953

Ludwig Bemelmans [Ferargil] is still the same knight errant progressing through the Europe he continues to adore in a manner which, despite all its charm and grace, has become (probably through a refusal to change in what he has recognized as a changing world) just a little aged. The same head waiters, the same Madame et Monsieur, the same enchanting harbor, this time Ischia, the same permanent landscape of the Riveria, Monte Carlo, remain what he knows and still cares to paint. The pictures are as good as possible, and still better than almost anyone else's who is interested in the same scenery, but the humor is slightly less divine.

January 1953

Stephen Etnier, *Shore Road*, 1951.

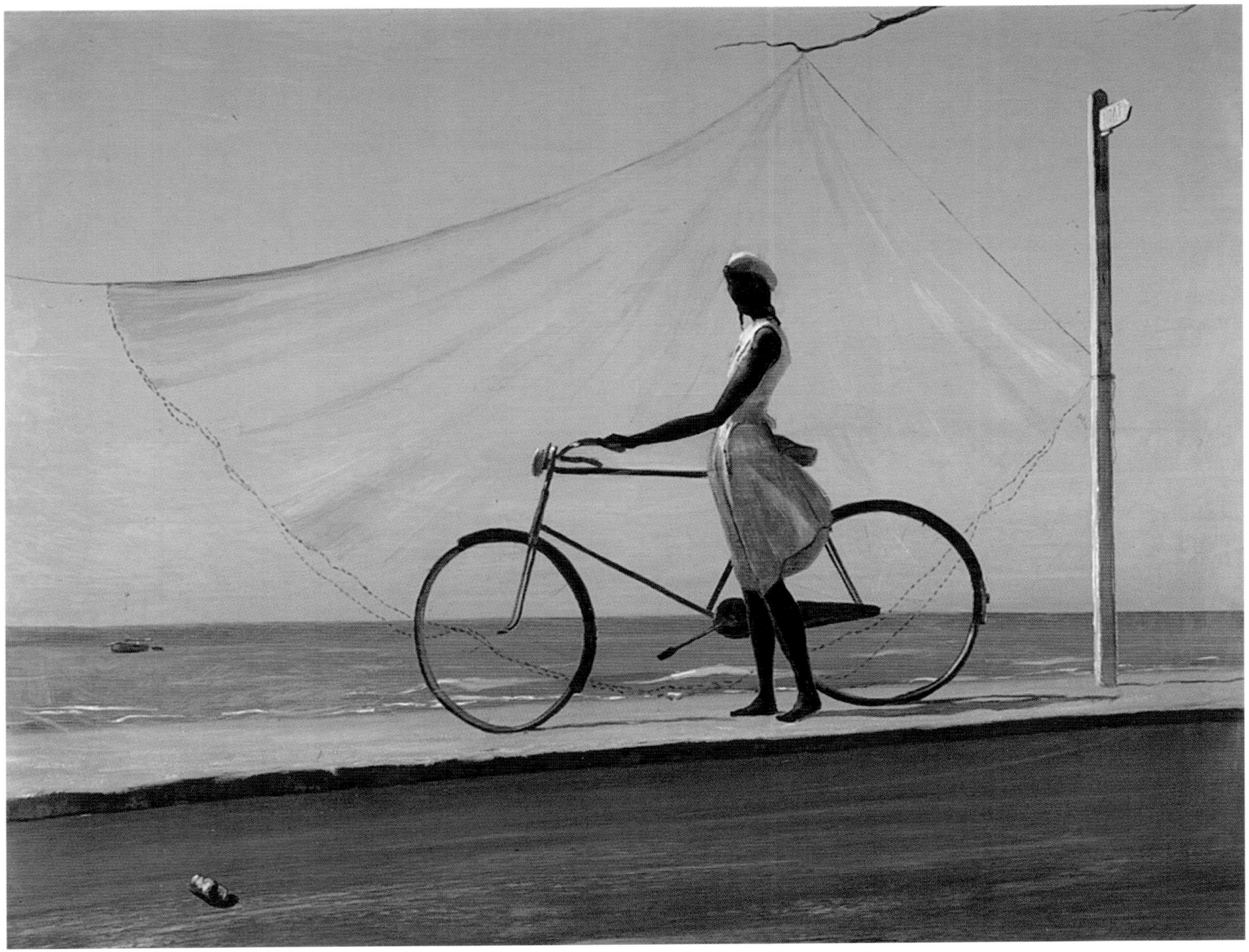

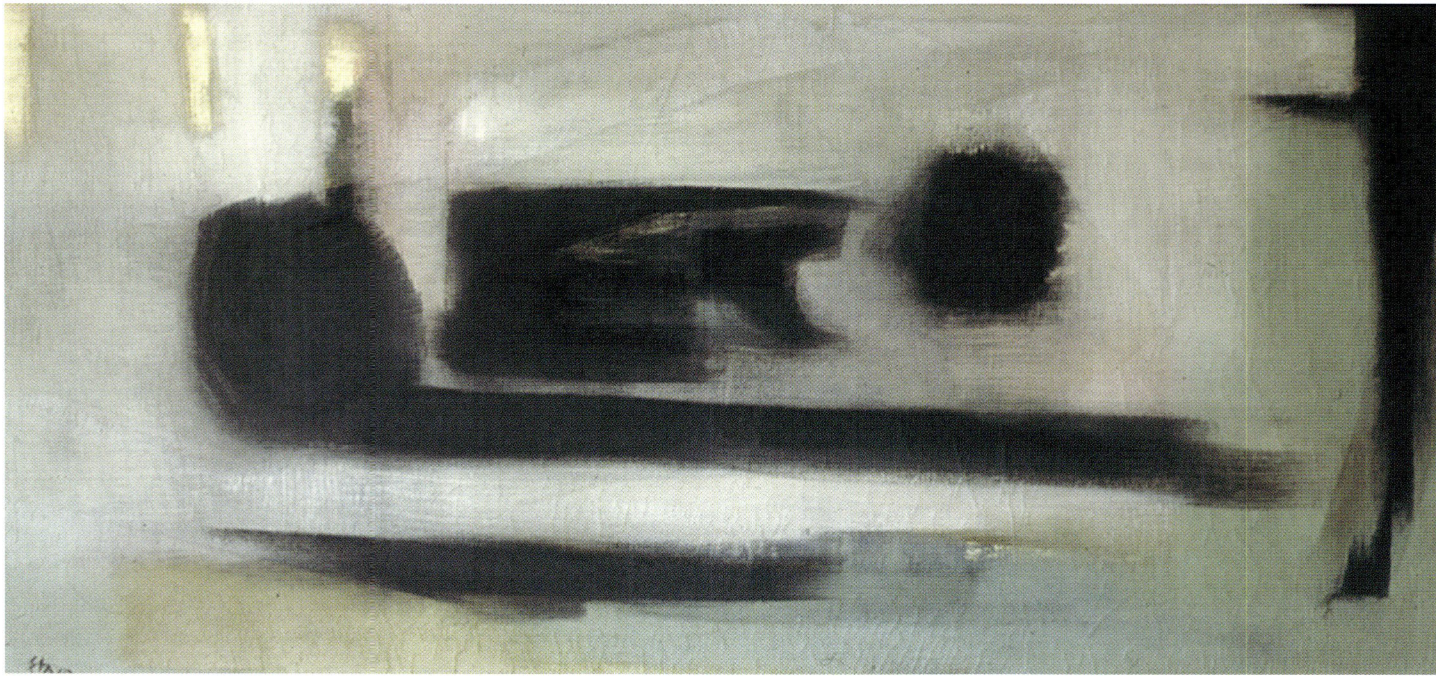

Theodore Stamos, *Tea House*, 7, ca. 1950.

Ludwig Bemelmans, *At Maxim's*, ca. 1950.

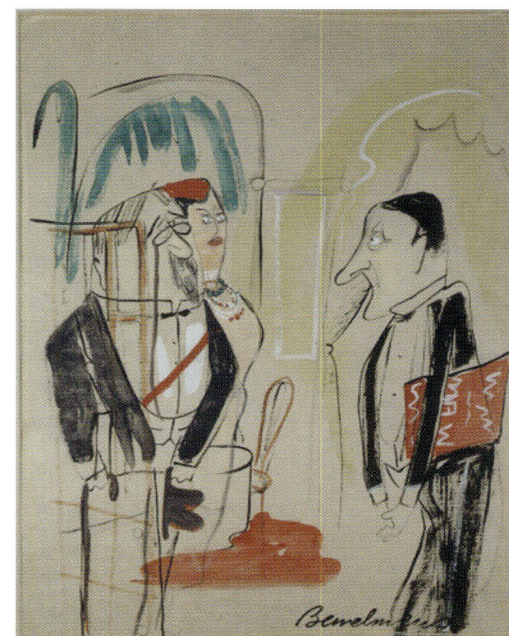

John Wilde's [Hewitt] latest pictures, with the exception of his still-lifes, have a wise lewdness which appears to be characteristic of many Surrealists after they have been painting seriously in this manner for any length of time. *Surprise* allows us to look at a lovely red-haired lady, slightly pregnant, and beautifully painted from the viewpoint of sin triumphant; the victory of lively sin over morality is elsewhere predominant. *Radishes* and *Smelts* have all the exquisiteness of semi-historical painting, and, like Dali, Wilde is a master of line and detail.

January 1953

Edward John Stevens, Jr. [Weyhe] has been travelling in Greece, Crete and Italy and in his latest work has attempted to condense the historical past of these countries through symbolical characters and settings. Thus, a gouache, *A Venetian Evening*, pictures a canal with an ancient craft, antique people and a Byzantine city rising in the background. *Night Over Phaistos* shows a figure of antiquity from which stems the empty ruins of Greece. His technique is based on Persian and primitive painting and frequently the painting is appealing and clever. Often his combinations of ancient methods, plus a washed Japanese-like background, come off as a tour-de-force, rather than actual painting.

February 1953

Master Drawings [J. Seligmann] coincides with the big museum drawing shows and brings together both well known artists and those who are still relatively uncommon in America. Beginning with Antoine Caron and the sixteenth century, continuing through La Hyre, Le Sueur, Mellan and Vouet, all of whose work illustrates the skill and accomplishment of drawing in a period in which artists were accepted as natural products of court life, a high point is reached in *Christ at Gethsemane* by Giandomenico Tiepolo—a somber, religious drawing in which there is an exquisite balance between landscape and the figures. The nineteenth century includes two drawings and a watercolor by Bonington. They are delicate, near-romantic, yet firmly controlled. *The Battle Field* by Géricault, in which space and color are handled in a highly beautiful and romantic manner, is perhaps the most unsuspected reward of the exhibition; and Gustave Moreau's almost difficult *Galatea* is a work to which a painter such as Rouault would turn—its heavily charged color and symbols now seem almost Surrealist. The twentieth century is represented by a Leger *Diver* which has extraordinary mass movement in a small space, the figure plunging directly into the foreground; a classical *Pierrot* by Picasso; a Redon, *Profile at Right*, in which an elaborate design to the far right of the drawing sets up a tension between the fragile, *spirituel* profile of a woman as seen dimly in a glass; and Seurat's *Bridge at Courbevoie* a dark, thickly drawn sketch which might well be a painting.

March 1953

Ludwig Y. Wolpert [Jewish Museum] a teacher at the Bezalel School, Palestine, and the foremost Israeli craftsman, exhibits ritual art objects. Wolpert is unique among his fellow craftsman in his use of Hebrew letters as architectural motifs. Thus in his crown for the Torah, Hebrew characters, changed so that each line is equal in width to the other, form a highly satisfactory design for the ancient crown. The effect is that of a simple yet dramatic cohesion between the past and the present. His work in silver and copper has an elegance which appears so natural that it has taken almost for granted until compared with the work of other craftsman. There are several mezuzoth that have an unusual delicacy combined with a deliberate break with more conventionally constructed objects, and this is true also of his Torah crowns.

Summer 1953

Gustav Wolf [Jacobi] German painter and engraver who took asylum in this country from the Nazi regime and died while a teacher in Northfield, Mass., was given a memorial exhibition of his work. His paintings and woodcuts are expressive of the spiritual despair and need for spiritual reconciliation felt by so many artists in the Germany of his period. Distorted forms, angels, strange galaxies make up the chaotic worlds of his woodcuts and engravings for the books of Psalm and Genesis. And in his oil painting also, the work is not primarily painting for its own sake, but to find a meaning in the universe. The total concept is one of personal intensity which makes itself felt most clearly in the prints where the work is technically of a very high order.

November 1953

Norwegian Serigraphs [Serigraph] is a collection of the work of Norwegian graphic artists who, with the exception of Erling Merton, have never shown in this country before. Their serigraphs are much freer than the American work, more influenced by the Far East, and the colors have a delicacy and a lightness which is not often attempted here. Erling Merton's style is the closest to his American contemporaries and he shows a controlled use of the medium. His *Speilegg and Tulipanen* are delightful still-lifes, somewhat derivative of Matisse, but the color is lighter and the composition is personal. *Klovnen* by Finn Christensen shows the serigraph technique used to approximate oils; extremely intricate and decorative motifs perpetuate a sense of fable or story and have a charm which is not belied by his novel use of the medium. Hanna Jessen's *Kergmiker* is possibly more clumsy and amateurish in the medium than would be allowed here, but there is an expression, which manages to override any failure of technique. The exhibition is also an object lesson to Americans working with serigraphs who have perhaps lost their originality though too strict an adherence to the problems of craft.

Summer 1953

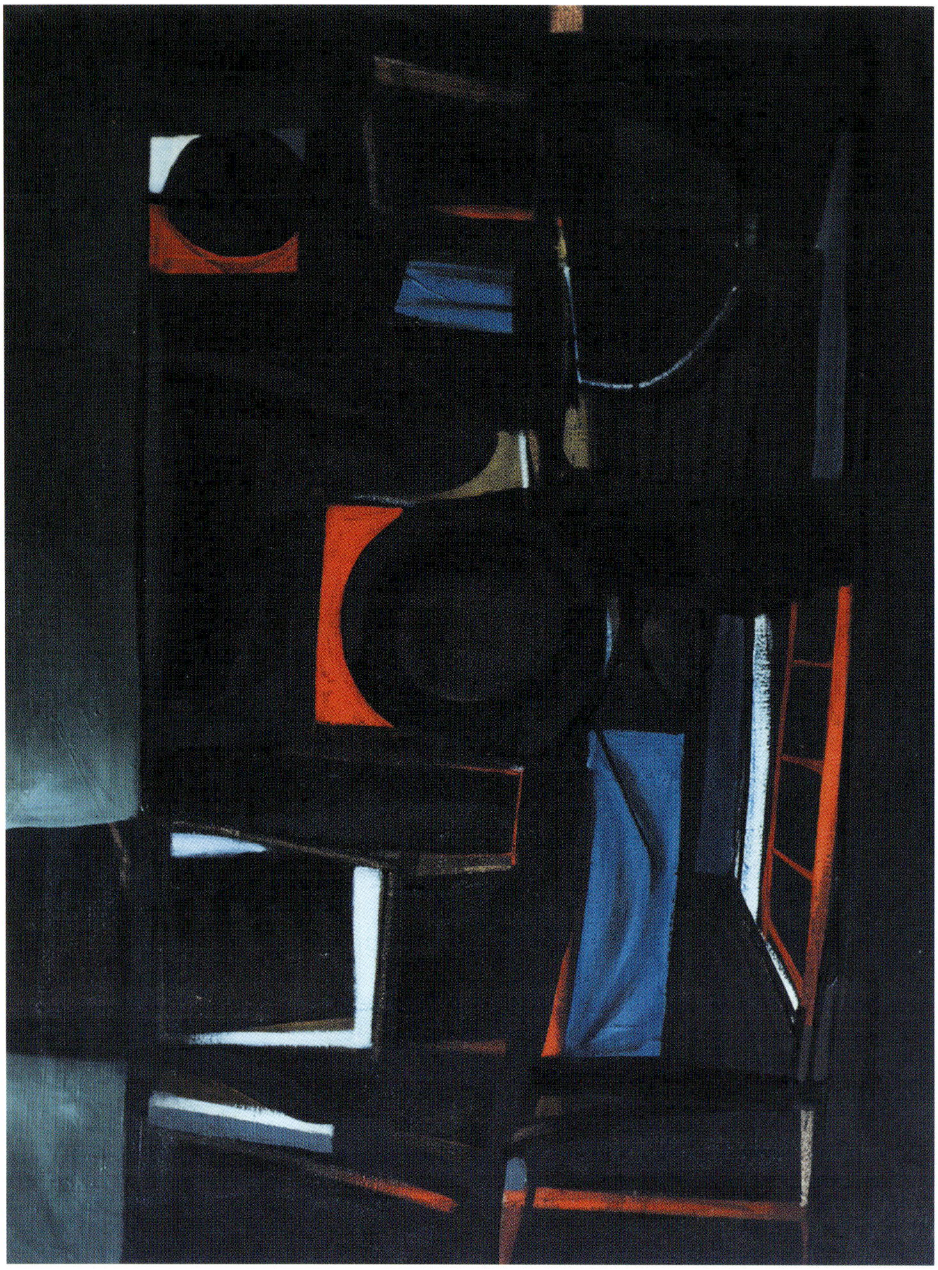

John Hultberg, *Embarkment*, 1953.

Richard Stankiewicz, *Tantrum for a Feeble Figure*, 1951.

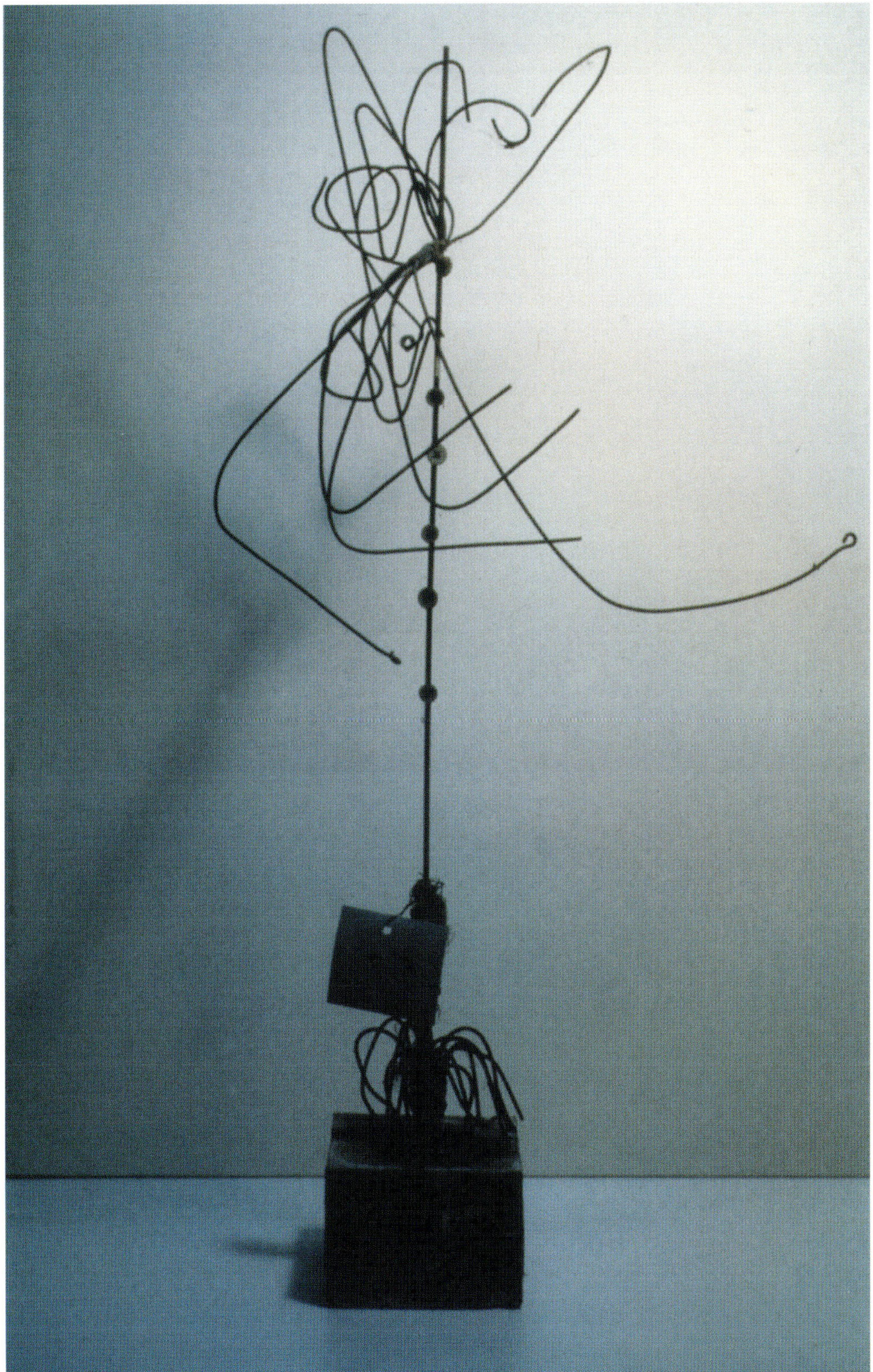

New York Society of Women Artists [Riverside Museum] recently had their annual exhibition. Most of the work was contemporaneous and this attitude gave the collection a sparkle which is frequently missing from such large groupings. Also, the direct femininity of the painting was less apparent than is usual and could be detected only in a tendency which most of the painters had to catch a particular moment in time, or to portray the particular atmosphere of a setting. And this sort of sensitivity, of course, is feminine and gave an additional aura to such paintings as *Kentucky Spring* by Ann Cole Phillips and *Remembered Moments* by Sylvia Carawe. *Fugue* by Lily Shuff and Frances Avery's *Vernal Patch* were two paintings of interest as was *Summer Storm* by Grace Borgenicht, whose work is very delicate, yet still a little too mannered. The sculpture was much duller, with the exception of Louise Nevelson's *Head of a Distant Relative*, reminiscent of Barbara Hepworth.

December 1953

Alfonso Ossorio's [Parsons] large show of recent paintings held several surprises. Not only were there many pictures of his vegetable, mineral and unconscious world, darkened and thinned, remote and complicated, but very new, brightly colored paintings wherein form was brought from the unconscious straight into the light of day. These new works mark a change in his style. It is as if everything that had gone on before was suddenly clarified—the whole multiple world of his art had found a direct meaning. His pictures had never wandered intangibly in their aura, but now they explode with a control that is quite delightful to witness, and with color which appears to be the reverse image of the color he had previously used. *Numbers 10* and *12* are large, direct statements of where the artist is at this point. Yet Ossorio's forms never appear arbitrary, but decisive; color precedes directly and the two combine in painting which leaves one alert to its further development.

January 1954

Enrico Donati [Parsons] continues his post-Surrealist experiments with roughened, velour-like surfaces, still somber in grays, blacks and white with an occasional earth color to brighten the scene. *Moonscape Black and Black* is indeed a trip to the moon, here a blackened crater. *Composition in Gray* contains several surfaces, heavy against light, and this painting in which there is breath and more uncontrolled atmosphere is perhaps the most successful of the group.

February 1954

Richard Lindner [Parsons], a German-born painter who lived for some time in Paris and now teaches at the Pratt Institute, has his first one man show in America. These paintings, looking back upon the Surrealist symbols, have a separate style, personally derived from the painter's own memories and concept of life. They contain the silence of the transfigured moment which is arrived at within Surrealist painting, yet they move backwards and forwards in time which is not static, but moves as the emotions themselves change. Having spent his childhood in a medieval city, Lindner places medieval rooms upon his canvas, closed rooms with low ceilings wherein appear, in *Entre-Acte*, the King of Bavaria seated upon a stool, the artist as a boy in a sailor suit, his aunt in early century dress, two friends inhabiting a space with which they are unfamiliar, yet made at ease by their position within the picture; this, his latest painting, has the strength of intuition brought to its most mature stage. *Proust* and *Verlaine* are painted with a sympathy which does not go beyond the private atmosphere of these artists, and thus the pictures affect us as memoirs in which personal fictions can be completely understood.

February 1954

Moura Chabor [Galerie Moderne] who has studied and painted in Paris, is showing here for the first time. Much admired by Bourdelle and influenced by Valadon, her painting has both inventiveness and charm, with neither quality lessening the other. Her color is that of the city, transplanted with only the relativity of time onto canvas, nothing else, no school or genre, has intervened. *L'Opera* appears just as it would to the practiced eye of one who views it suddenly, for the first time, at exactly the moment for which he has been prepared. It is perhaps this kind of realism which has never quite presented itself in American painting, realism which is fictional as well as representational, that separates her work from her other painters of the Paris scene.

February 1954

Cuno Amiet [St. Etienne] Swiss artist known there as the "Painter of Sunny Life," has his first exhibition in America. Studying in Paris in 1888 under Bouguereau, he was later influenced by Bernard and Sérusier who brought him into contact with the work of Gauguin and Van Gogh. This exhibition, with the exception of an early picture, *Red Earth,* 1924, contains the work of recent years. Surprisingly enough, little change seems to have appeared. He is an Impressionist in *Still-life with Apples. Pasture,* 1949, closely resembles the Gauguin-like *Red Earth*. Quality and interest vary tremendously, yet the pictures are successful in a simplified way. He is indeed sunny; there are no problems. It appears that once one has mastered the technique of the 1890's as Amiet did, an unlimited amount of canvases may be produced. Viewing this painting as the work of a Swiss, a good bit of this tranquillity and satisfaction may be understood. It is the work of a man who carried his knowledge with him from Paris, and then proceeded to paint in isolation.

March 1954

Alfonso Ossorio, *Add and Multiply*, 1954.

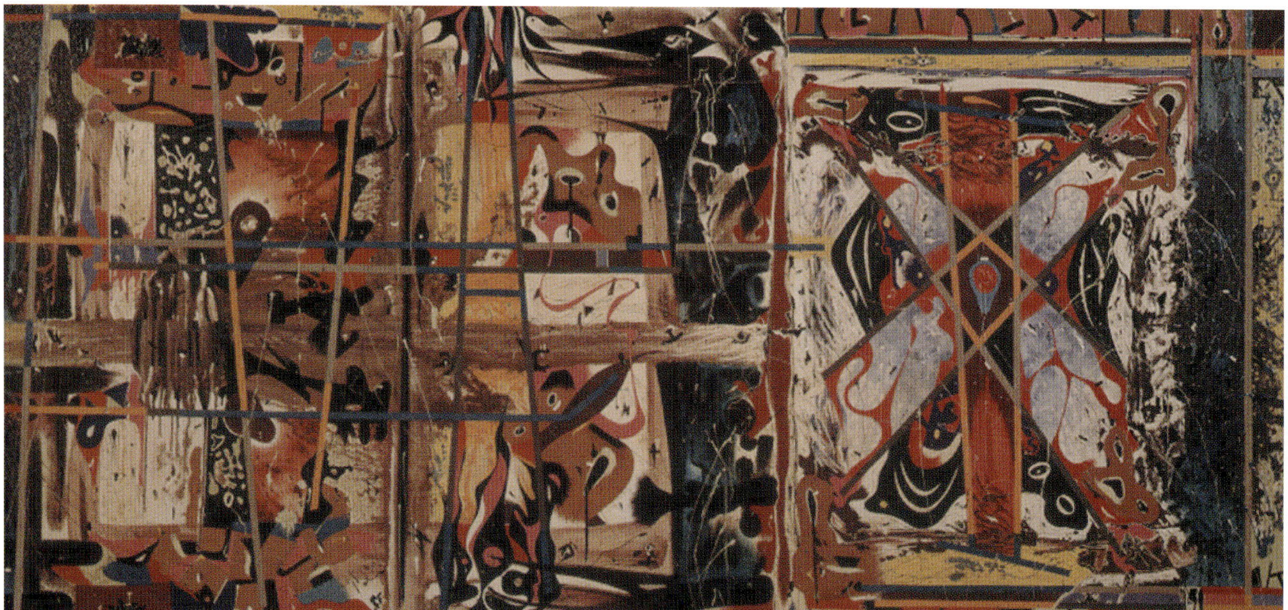

Enrico Donati, *Composition in Gray*, 1950.

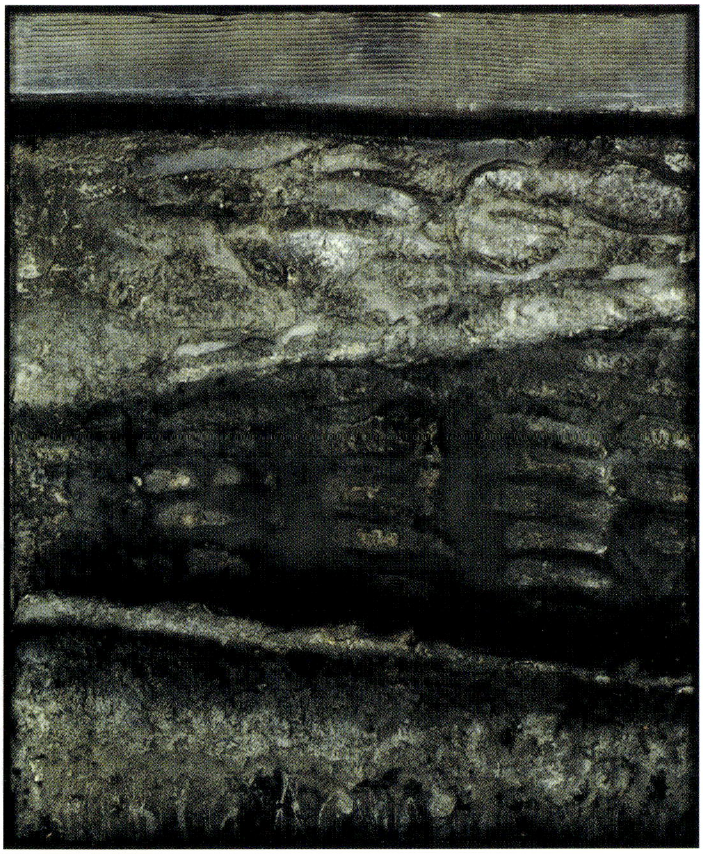

Moura Chabor, *Children With Nuns*, ca. 1950.

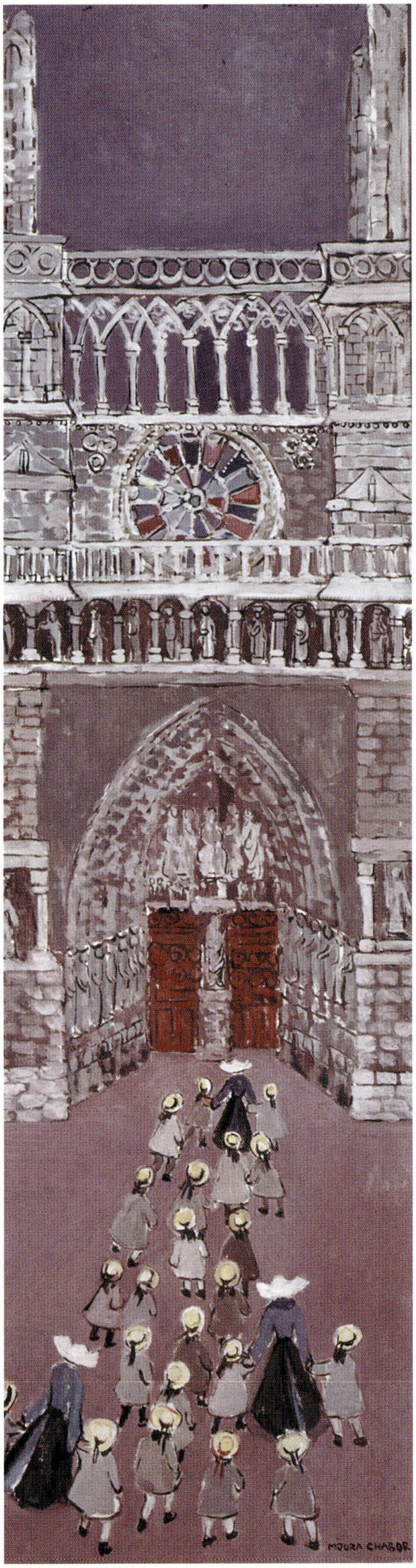

Louise Nevelson [Clapp] showed recent sculpture in terra cotta, wood and marble. She has constructed, with several pieces of terra cotta joined together by a cylinder, sophisticated primitives who are capable of movement and even appear prepared to speak. *Mountain Woman* in aluminum has the planes and abbreviations of Cubism—as to a degree does all her work—and *River* in terra cotta proves that even Maillol can be abbreviated without a lessening of power or beauty. In *Twilight Figure* she has chosen marble to render a figure in mysterious contemplation, cubed and curved, and here her sense of deletion is apparent where after many choices only the essential plane is allowed to appear. This sculpture is one of varied and shaded meaning of half-tones, ironic and beautiful.

May 1954

Alfred Leslie [de Nagy] has left behind those startling still-life abstractions of his last show and following the current trend exhibits paintings of the figure. What remains is still a sudden use of carmine, of bright green falling from the shadows of his blacks, grays and madders. What is left behind is a virtuosity and daring which are his real forte, an ease and looseness which carry him out of the threatening monotony of this present show into the foreground of artistry. These pictures are all studies of a seated female figure painted with many slashing strokes to remove any static possibility. In *The Black Stockings*, *The Black Shadow*, we find thus a series of virtuoso experiences on canvas, but we do not have the seated female figure. She moves from picture to picture farther outside the painter's reach, so that finally one wonders where the original intent existed. Leslie appears to have been doing several things at once, with one eye on the figure and the other fixed on his mobile attitude toward art itself, a difficult separation. This often leads, as here, to painting about painting where the real experience never quite comes off. Extremely successful is a series of brilliant floral pictures, probably the best by a contemporary now on view in New York.

May 1954

Younger American and European Painters [Jackson] is a refreshing exhibition made up of the work of painters who have been introduced previously in New York shows. The outstanding painters, for this reviewer, are William Scott and Lawrence Calcagno. Scott, an Englishman, whose work at first glance looks like that of New York painters shown recently at the large Stable Gallery gathering, separates himself by certain European mannerisms and methods of applying paint; and, despite his entirely different style, his most subtle relationship is to the English painters, Sutherland and Bacon. Calcagno, an American who now lives in Paris, shows *Red Painting*, an abstraction whose merit depends to a large degree on the artist's excellent color values and his understanding of spatial composition. Hultberg is an abstractionist with powerful compositional drives which perform here most favorably in *Sea Journey*. Trukes, well-known in Germany, shows several idioms, one remarkably like the present French abstractionist style derived from Impressionism and another, strictly German in its formal shapes and linear design.

June 1954

Nachum Gutman [Heller], who lives in Israel, exhibits watercolors which are whimsical, imaginative renderings of the Israeli scene. He is also an illustrator and these pictures might well be shown in storybook form. Light, amusing, the houses and beaches have the atmosphere of a fairy tale which may be quite real to the occupants of the land. There is a holiday or holy day spirit present in these pictures—he has removed any somber reminders of the past or future.

June 1954

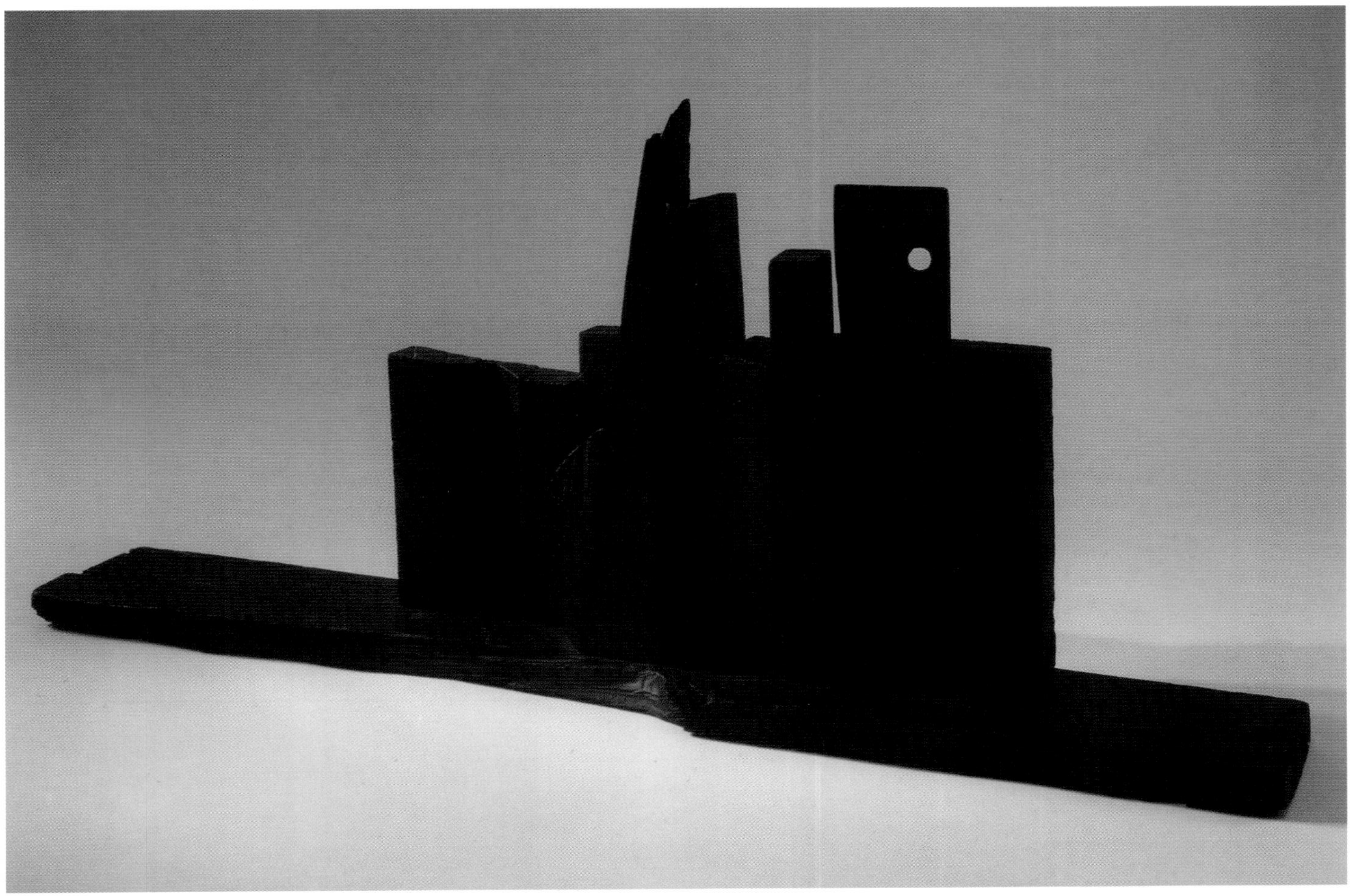

Louise Nevelson, *Moon Spikes*, 1953. © 2002 Estate of Louise Nevelson / Artists Rights Society (ARS), New York.

Alfred Leslie, ca. 1950.

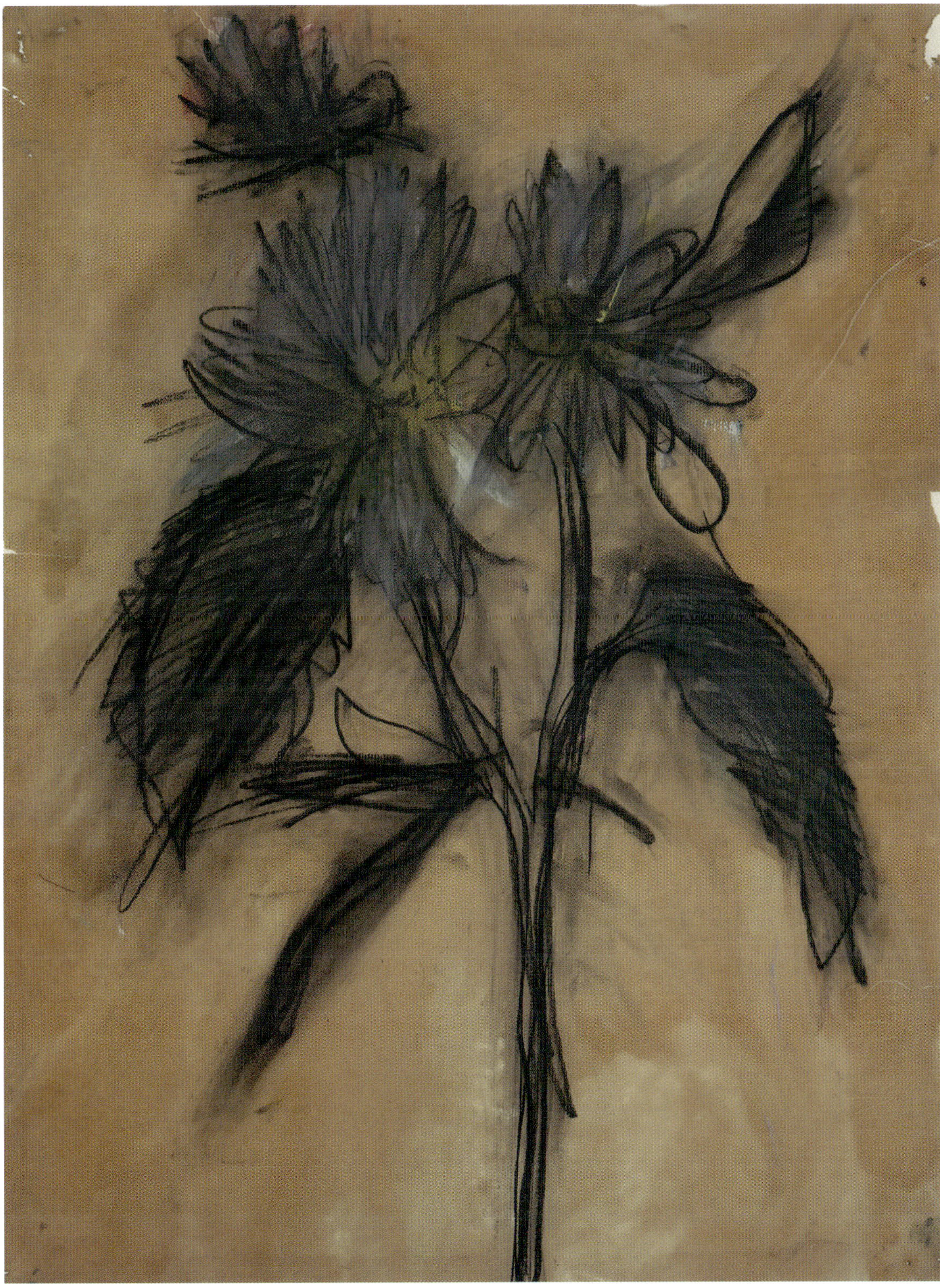

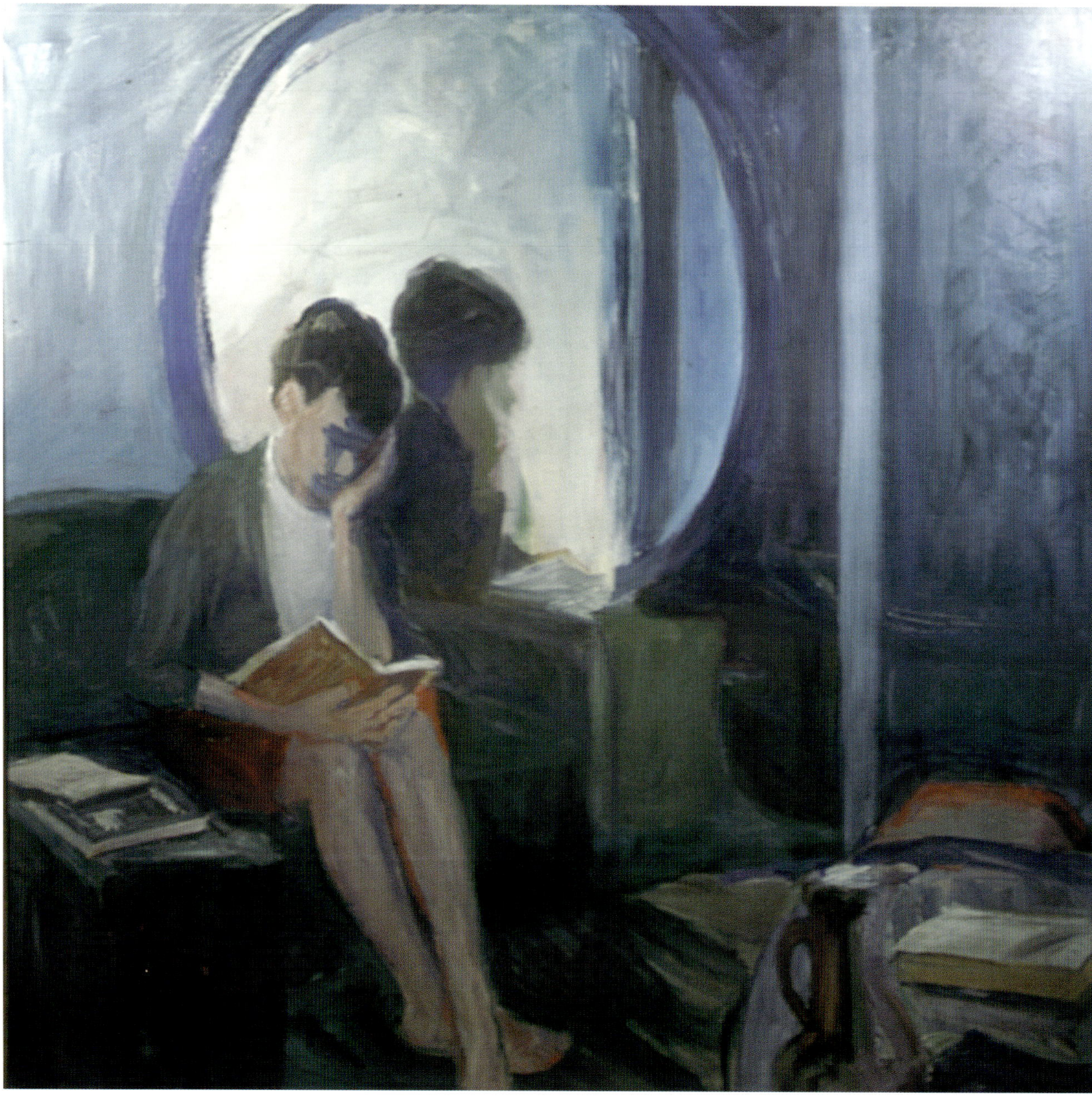

June Felter, *Girl Reading*, 1963.

This retrospective of June Felter's work from the 1960s gave us a privileged view of the painting of an artist whose work came to flower during the heyday of Bay Area figurative painting. The show also underscored the tactical error committed by not including her in the exhibition of Bay Area Figuration currently launched on a national museum tour (*A.I.A.*, Nov. 1990): Felter represents the movement in one of its most lucid, glowing aspects, and she certainly holds her own in the company of Park, Diebenkorn and Bischoff.

Girl Reading, from Felter's 1963 period (well-represented here), shows her painterly sensitivity; in this work, as elsewhere, she maintains an impressive control over detail, lavishing paint upon certain areas, while never permitting them to overwhelm the larger composition. Felter possesses an inborn fluency that is particularly evident in the reach of her color. Fluency, of course, may be the distinguishing characteristic of Bay Area painting, but Felter takes it a step further than many of her peers: she never stops to "stage-direct" a given picture. This is not quasi-narrative painterly choreography.

In the smaller acrylic paintings also presented here she uses paint as if it were watercolor—giving it a commensurate speed and luminosity. In fact, it is to be noted how very much at home she is in these quotidian studies, giving their surfaces an authority that transcends their ostensibly mundane subject matter. The faces in the subjects in *Woman in Blue* and *Man with White Hair Seated* are built up in a way we associate with David Park—that is, color glows through successive layers. Felter's work is tactile in a possessive manner; "I have so intimately touched this," she seems to be saying, "that it belongs to me." In this respect *Ironing* is one of the stars of the show. The ironer's simple dress, with its many ranges of color and layered white, suggest a Degas dancer's tutu. The painter does not glamorize her subject to the point of forgetting the concentration demanded by the task depicted. The woman's dress, in its nest of color, is pushed up against the ironing board, and, as she presses down upon her iron, we are aware of the weight brought to bear in the process. This implied identification of the artist with her subject is obviously instinctive; it brings a poignant new dimension to the painting.

These and other strategies of observation consistently concern themselves with a domestic circle—family, friends—pursuing daily life. Not surprisingly, Felter has been criticized (like Berthe Morisot) for being a painter of the "bourgeois" scene. This tarnished attitude has no relevance. This is good painting.

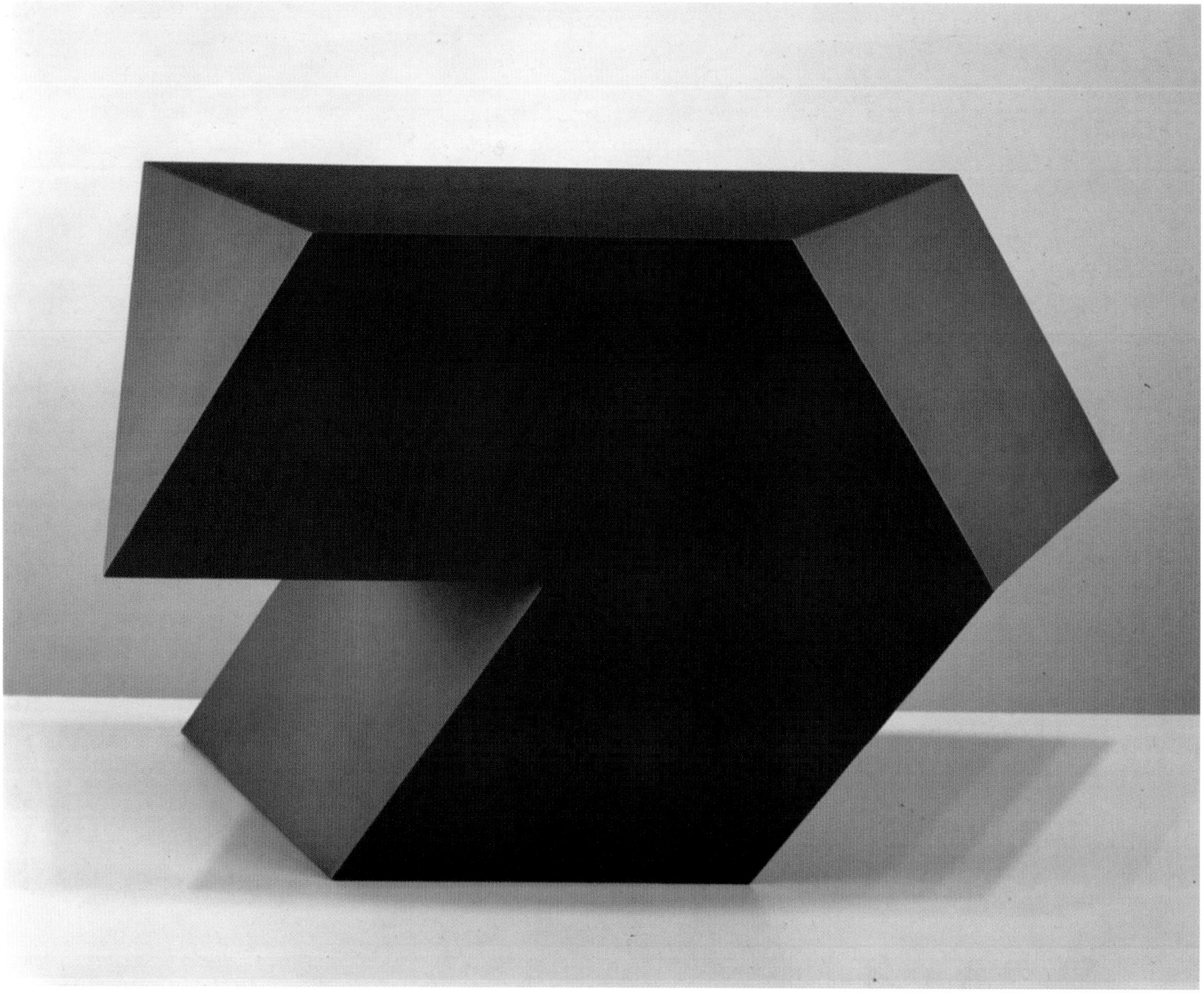

Tony Smith, *Tau*, 1965.

EGYPT
[*for* Tony Smith]

Because nobody knew whether it was Monday or Tuesday
the park that was on Monday began on Tuesday

This water flows either ways with exceptions
for blue moments described as loaded when

Never to make a remark about merely a generous lump
leaves no ivy over your tough Pharaoh meter

Either liked to parade in front of mirrors
going underground was a busy strike so that

When examined the bird's tread went which way
and that the pastime was being amazed

And getting out the size of the hump

The storage space it occupied "simple, very
authoritative, very enduring things."

A vigorous antiquity into which the slab was
inserted and either said not enough in spite of

The ribbons of oozes nobody made an oasis
out of it until dissatisfactions

With sizes more confusing than the tomb
where zero unwraps Ouch! you've printed my thumb

You have lost the original which was perhaps
better but the boys did their best lying on the

Mowed grass whispering butter as a matter of fact

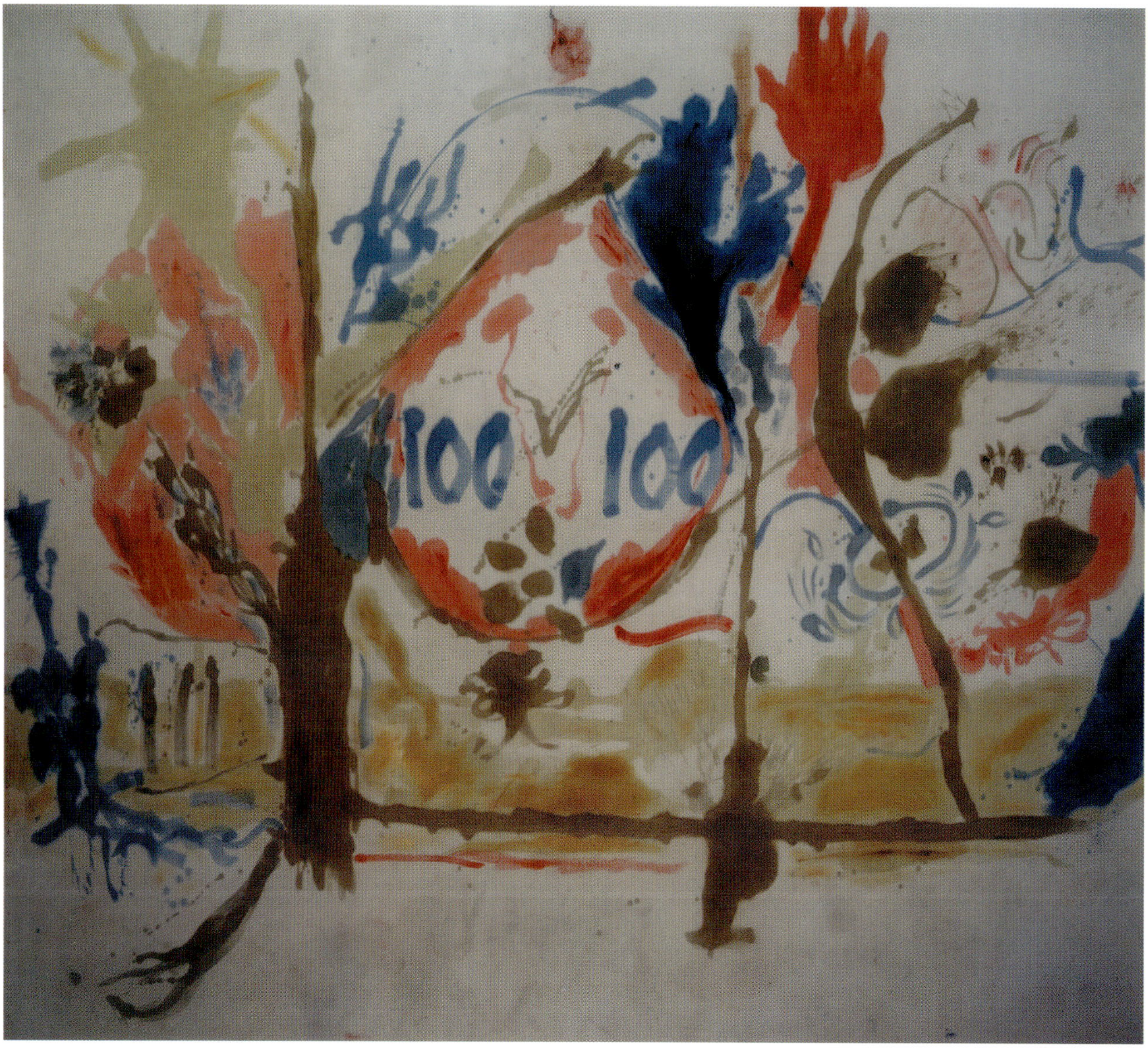

Helen Frankenthaler, *Eden*, 1957.

Helen Frankenthaler: The Moment and The Distance

Helen Frankenthaler has been active throughout her career in bringing us up to date. When she was a member of the early Tibor de Nagy Gallery in the 1950's, her position was separate from that of her colleagues who had located themselves as "Second Generation Abstract Expressionists." In that gallery, not that she wasn't absorbing the same atmosphere, going to the same parties, but her eye was focused differently. Eschewing the de Kooning-Franz Kline axis, her influences are to be found closer to Kandinsky, Marin, Pollock. She was an Expressionist because she applied the emotional and physical techniques to the canvas that were shared by her colleagues. Later, following the example of Pollock, her canvas was placed on the floor. She adapted, quite naturally, Pollock's drip technique which required a different physical involvement.

The Retrospective of 1969 at the Whitney Museum, organized by E. C. Goosen, offered us painting from periods in the artist's early career continuing to 1969. The current exhibition at the Corcoran Gallery, Washington, D.C., under the supervision of Gene Baro, is concerned with the paintings from 1969 through 1974.

Several critics have suggested the influence of Arthur Dove, which she steadfastly denies. If, as Hilton Kramer has explained, the art of Dove is that of "lyrical meditation," we can agree with Frankenthaler. I can see no parallel idea in their attitude. One might assume in an exhibition at this point in her career there would be more meditative aspects. Not at all. The quality silence portends is rejected.

A product of her own generation and the milieu she occupies, Frankenthaler consistently relies on excitement in the moment of transition of brush to—the canvas. We are aware in her painting of an ambition to create something new. The moment the brush touches down the painter is free to explore. The brush carries the momentum as the artist explores the moment—moment and momentum are the springboards. Color possibly leads the way into the canvas—Frankenthaler is a colorist, as was Dove, but for her, color is the access to excitement rather than meditation. What she sees, feels, after a necessary moment of gestation goes immediately into the canvas. One does not observe normal quiet here. Detachment—yes, in the middle of the struggle one is aware of detachment, a stepping back from the canvas, as a critical eye views it.

Action, sophistication, intelligence, an interesting combination of assets make up the attitude of a city person who is called a "landscape artist." Does she make that transposition? I am not certain of this. Her landscapes exist on the margin of her universe. She forces Nature to copy Art.

These paintings are landscapes of the interior. Circe lives on Frankenthaler's island, translated into Manhattan. *Venus Revealed*, is Venus Observed from an artist's studio.

This exhibition shows that Frankenthaler forces difficult options upon herself. She is not going to paint from Art History. She is not going to paint *en plein air*, or a still life. These decisions would place heavy burdens on the arts, they are not her forte, she is interested in going somewhere else. Her painting requires an intense dramatization of the self—as in those paintings of Jackson Pollock, who may be said to influence her—particularly in the positions of canvases on the floor—in the destruction of normal positions for approach to paintings. It has been remarked elsewhere that her intelligence is active in the positioning of the canvas, in the shrewdness of the lyrical passages. She has given herself freedom to apply the unconscious. This unconscious is another brush.

How then to account for her references? Her main reference, I would say, is Surrealism. Surrealism gives her freedom, permits her to behave on the canvas in any manner she wishes, so long as she has control of her brush and is only motivated by the Surrealist impulses in painting, Frankenthaler is thus visually freed, and this counts for much of her extravagance, her impulsiveness in playing with another idea on the surface of the canvas, disturbing the environment, so the painting is never dull.

In this lively Corcoran exhibit we may note her critical eye, her attitude of self-appraisal, arriving out of cool air to be metamorphosed into any temperature she chooses. She is painting a series of surprises, and called them "interior landscapes." References to Hans Hoffman are not out of order.

The "coltishness," to borrow a word from Barbara Rose which showed up in *Eden* (1957) has disappeared, but not the wit of that painting. *Mountains and Sea* (1951) a seminal painting, a real breakthrough, has progeny, although they do not surpass that exceptional, seminal painting. There are more classical structures, *Nature Abhors a Vacuum, The Sound of the Bassoon*. The sudden joke, the derring-do, are not dissipated. Probably there are less happy accidents in the work, more decisions.

The moment now becomes the distance.

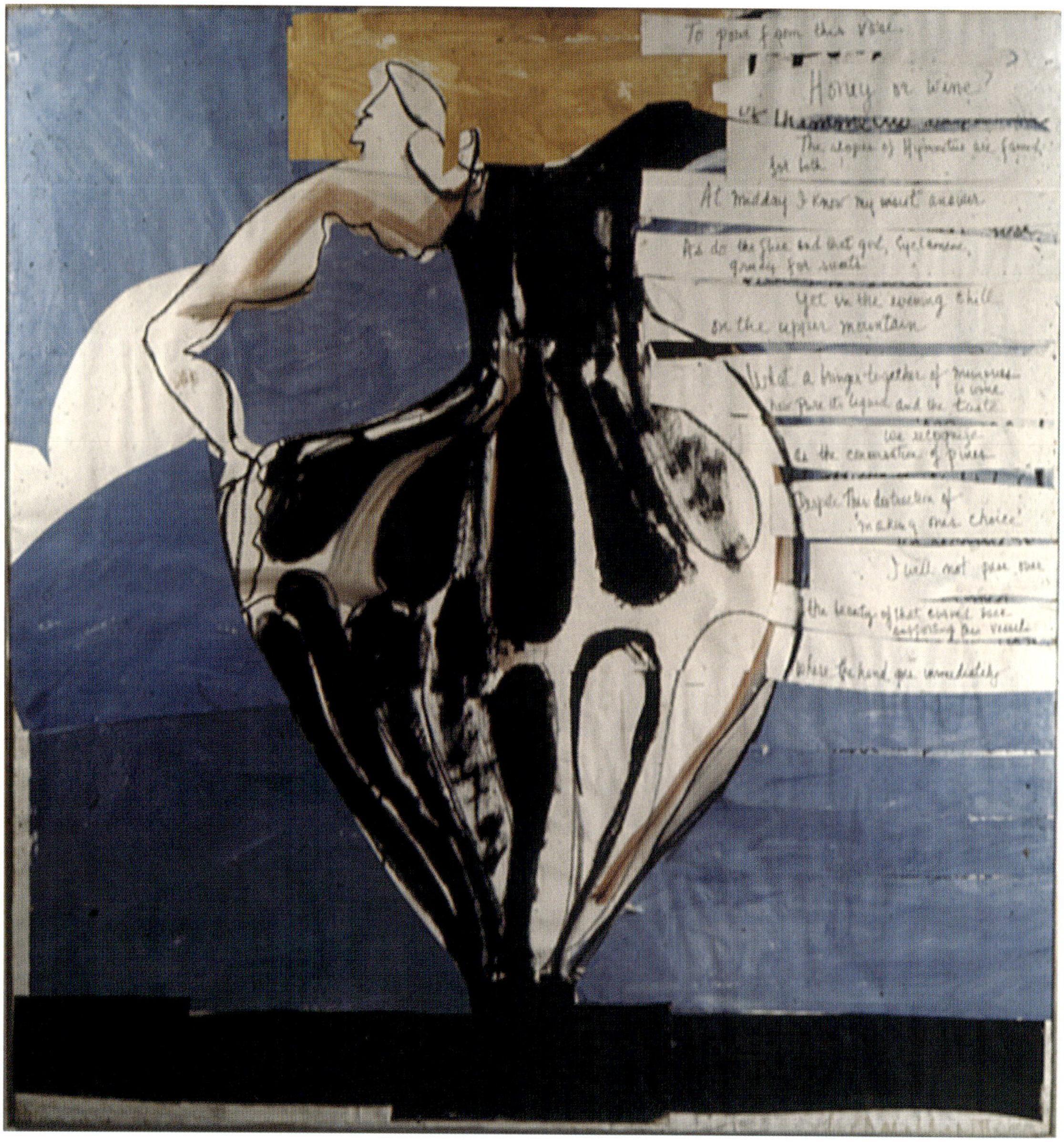

Mary Abbott, with a poem by Barbara Guest, *Honey or Wine?*, 1971.

This collaboration on paper was made in the Southampton, Long Island, N.Y., studio of Mary Abbott in 1971. I had recently returned from Greece, and we were in her huge studio above the little ponds and reeds that led to the sea in Southampton. I was attempting to describe the artifacts I had seen in Greece, and to convey an atmosphere of the Greek Islands I had absorbed.

As Mary's trapeze swung on the rafters above us, she brought out several art books on Greece, in particular one of vases, and the black surface of Greek mirrors. For weeks she drew and I wrote, and together we created our own artifacts.

She drew the vase, and then she asked me to write a poem about the vase. Looking at the vase prompted me to suggest she attach strips of paper, that she "collage" the sides of her drawings, by cutting out strips of paper on which I would write parts of a poem which she could then attach to the drawing. We called our collaboration, *Honey or Wine?*

I preferred this invention, rather than writing a lone poem "about" the vase. I wished the poem to look as if it were attached to the vase, as the studio had now become attached to a foreign surface. By now there were several of our personally crafted works, even paintings with poems inscribed on them.

It was a year in the history of American Art when artists and poets responded to, and were encouraged by, the enormous activity in the arts that surrounded them.

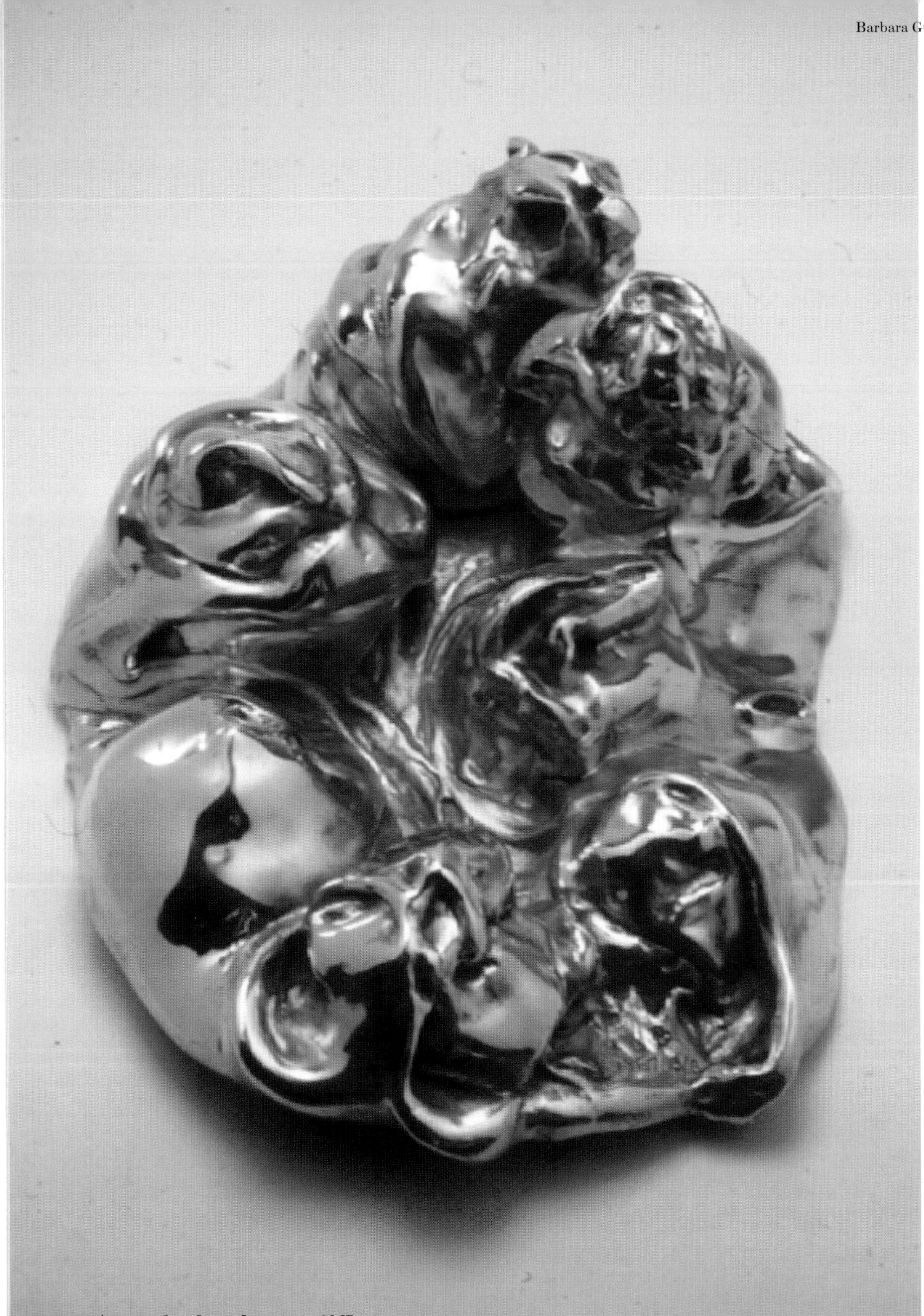

Louise Bourgeois, *End of Softness*, 1967.

"Why has Louise Bourgeois finally become the Artist of the moment?"

"I don't like people who aren't angry."
Louise Bourgeois

All over the world museums are acquiring her work. She is now considered the "phenomenon" of the decade and will represent us at the Venice Biennale as she did at Documenta IV. And yet, is she truly the "artist of the *moment*?"

Louise Bourgeois has never let go of the initial subjects from which she composed in her youth. As she tells us, "for more than fifty years I have been talking about the same subject so I have a consistency." Obsessively she reviews the stages of her life and their emotional accompaniment as the subject of her art. One after another her sculptures present themselves as figures from her life history or commentary on her emotional life with its secret deposits. She says, "I feel the ambivalence in everything. I try to visualize it and to express the fragile center between extremes."

Today Bourgeois is compared to Marguerite Duras whose recapitulations of her history in her books and on the screen reflect the injuries and crises of her life. Also directly related to Bourgeois are the Proustian memories, the obsessions of Svevo, the work of Musil, and the labyrinthine Joyce, himself. For them, as for Bourgeois, the art form exists in the recapitulation. The past becomes a symbol, a guide, a revelation of experience never separated from an artist's permanent caress.

This caress of the past is not usual to a sculptor. The artist of the surface is employed by the demands of the surface. The genealogy of the surface has created its own sense of time. The sculptor must learn to condense time and permit the work to do its own replay in texture and modeling, the style which is advancing into the future even as the sculptor employs the tools. Yet Bourgeois resolves this necessity through her sense of intimacy, her sense of self, her obsessiveness if one wishes to call it that which permits her to retire into the timelessness of her own enclosures. She refuses the inherited romantic vision of sculpture as held in the great hand of a god, instead she transfers this vision to herself wherein lies her center of absorption.

In an era of fading dependence on modernity we now acclaim work that concentrates less on form within a spatial modality, but rather on forms that propose a speaking body, that "listen" to the body, that hear the body's alarms through new sculptural commands. There is a preference for a "dialogue" to develop between the sculptor and the subject, rather than to witness the loneliness of an art form in the process of creation.

The art of Bourgeois working in an indigenous way has undoubtedly had its influence on younger artists such as Kiki Smith who are resistant to both non-expressionist and modernist art forms. These experimenting artists are drawn to the excitement of Bourgeois' pioneering arrangement of her figures, her throwing pieces of her work into odd corners of the room, piling them up on top of each other

—she was stacking bricks of wood as if reaching for a formula long before conceptualists began to rearrange their tiles. Bourgeois was among the first to experiment with intricate arrangements and odd formations of materials. When she fashioned pieces from wire mesh and wrapped clay, she pointed out that there are uses for any material that comes to your hand; this radical experimentation has influenced sculptors not content with the forging of machine parts, or carving in marble, in search of other forms of expressiveness that afford a more inquisitive examination. Like the radical Frederick Kiesler, architect of the "Endless House" of whom she reminds us, and whose spirit of adventure matches Louise Bourgeois' own, she is outside her generation and has remained so, free roaming, displaced, until her work finds its home in the work of the young.

These experiments took place after she had given up painting. Her *Femme-Maison (Woman House)* paintings in which women have houses perched on their bodies in place of heads were taken up later by the feminist cause, and Bourgeois began to attend feminist meetings in the art world. Sculptural ideas began to come into the pictures. And then she gave up painting, because she became inhibited by it and she was not "satisfied by its level of reality." She needed an art that was more physical and tangible. "I could express much deeper things in three dimensions."

Bourgeois was among the first to present "performance" art, before the

Louise Bourgeois, *The Destruction of the Father*, 1974.

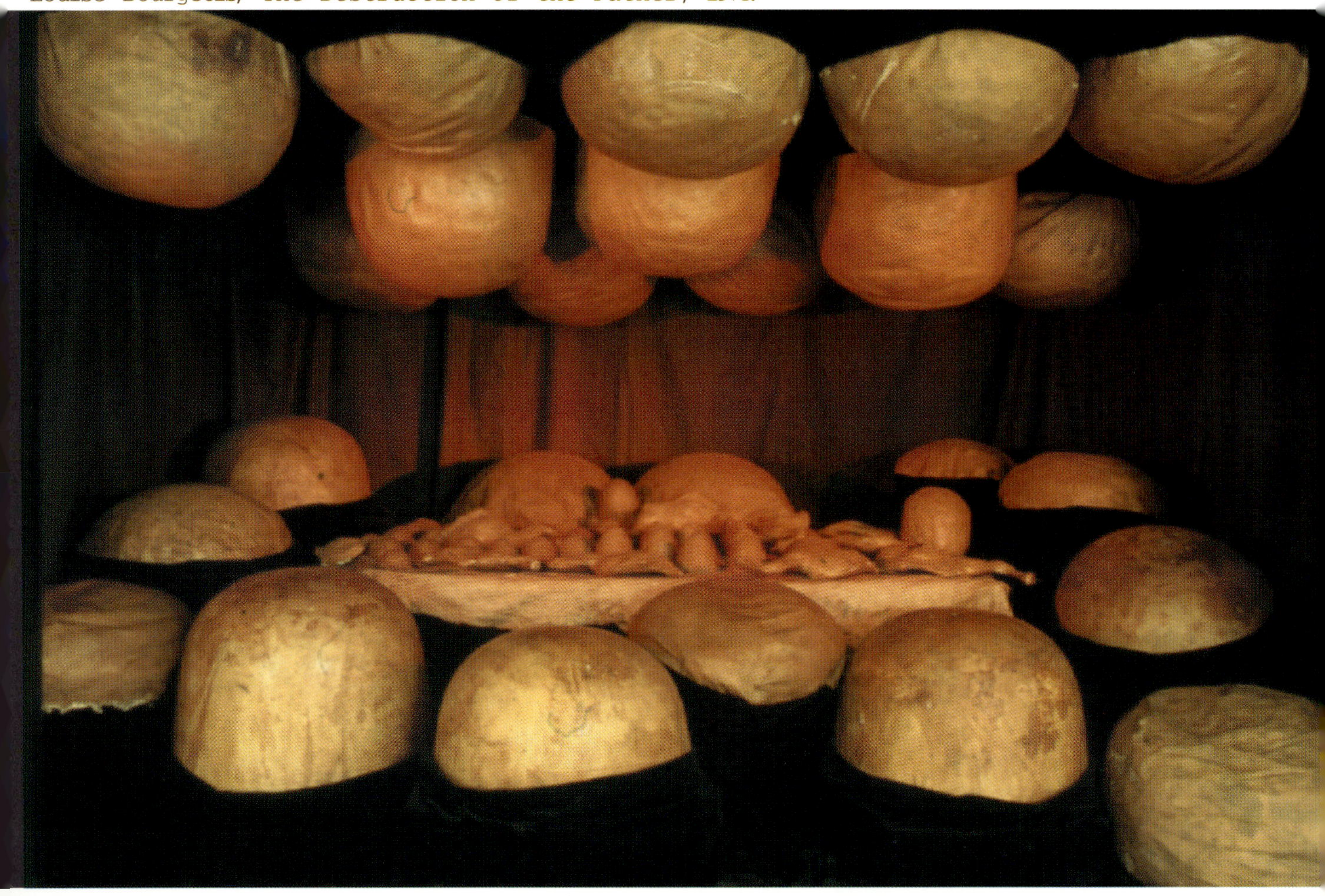

public had even heard of it. She is a natural performer, her work is highly "active" and indeed in a museum or gallery seems to cry out for more space to move around in. Also we can suspect that Louise Bourgeois, herself, likes to play dress-up. Photographs show her holding up looping breasts tacked all over her body, sculptural forms she used in her work. Her constructions, such as *Confrontation* (1978) demanded a participating audience.

She has worked her way through the influence of Surrealism, (as did Kiesler) developing other insights, using a Surrealism that exists in terms of her own identity. "Identity," she says, "I have too much Identity."

Her art, even on its most trembling and exposed base is a sophisticated art. When her plaintive persona approach the "lairs" she constructed, this civilized and highly intelligent artist is pretending that their primitivism and her witchcraft indicate a primordial sensibility.

Art Deco as an influence? Born in France and attending the university, only leaving for America upon her marriage to the eminent art historian, Robert Goldwater, evidences of this movement would have surrounded her. And in support of her admiration for this form she has created sculpture in terms of Art Deco. An abrupt surprise for the unsuspecting are the stunning Art Deco gates at the entrance to her Brooklyn studio. The thoughtfully titled, *The End of Softness*, (1967), refers to a period of "soft" sculptural material and is not, as this writer believed a "poetic title." Under the magic is a literal imagination. This flat sculpture now cast in bronze with waves of movement and molded plateaus, although expressionist in feeling, has the mood of Art Deco. *Fallen Woman*, (1981), compared to the puzzled figures clinging to their personalities of the 1940's is like a shower of Narcisse Noir. Bourgeois has the ability to take us unawares. Those totem-like early figures were followed in the 50's by leaf-like figures (*Brother and Sister*) that have an Art Deco velvet clinging to them.

The 1960's tell of an intimate struggle to release inhibiting emotions and their history is alarming. Her *Fillette* hangs like the common "file" bag French woman use for marketing, and one wonders if this is a word-play. There is the suspicion that this *Fillette* (young girl) is the sculptor encased in latex over which is poured plaster, and yet that is not the story, because another body may hang in the bag and perhaps the wicked suspect in the sculpture has to do with an incident in the life of the young Louise, etc. In the work of Bourgeois we learn to search for a hidden story, the sculptural forms in their physical wrapping take on a meaning outside of Art. And always we must watch out for her wit and when the wit reaches us it is likely to turn into candor that is startling.

Destruction of the Father made in 1974 with latex over plaster in which, Bourgeois first uses the concept of witness or spectator, rather than participant in what appears to be an event. But this "event" also celebrates the sculptor's revenge against her father. "I don't like people who aren't angry," she says.

After the death of her husband in 1972 her work was repeatedly "aggressive" as she cut and drilled pieces of wood ("like knitting"), but this aggressive work made her "doubt her femininity" and the materials she "dismembered" made her anxious. Plaster, wax, and latex, she says are friendly materials, bronze is "dead." When bronze is used in her casting, as in *The End of Softness*, the aspect of Art Deco is heightened.

Again and again Bourgeois uses sexual imagery. This is evident especially in *Cumuli I,* a late sixties piece where she first uses clusters of shapes like penises. *Woman-Maison (Woman House* '81*)* in highly polished marble is possibly the most challenging. She stacks the penis-like shapes one against the other and the taller ones appear to hold up the smaller ones until the eye begins to follow not the shape but the configuration in its entirety. Bourgeois offers this candid explanation: "The Phallus is the subject of my tenderness. It's about vulnerability and protection. After all I lived with four men, with my husband and three sons. I was their protector."

(The poet, Marianne Moore, also protected an obsessive world, that of the animal kingdom. Living beyond her generation, she received the country's attention, then she became a source, like Bourgeois, of ideas for a younger generation. She hid her bushel under a much photographed tri-cornered hat.)

Today, Bourgeois is frequently photographed in a cap. Not as one might expect, a gamin's cap, but a non-denominational hat that looks as if it belonged to the captain of a freighter in a Jean Gabin film. The eyes under the cap do not, like Moore, wear the gaze of a startled faun. After "fifty years of talking about the same subject," they are snappish and wise and haunted. The history of Louise Bourgeois confirms her words, although considering her feminist position the choice of the male pronoun is puzzling: "The artist does not go through the rites of passage . . . he remains a child that is not innocent. He is not able to liberate himself from the unconscious. It's a tragic fate."

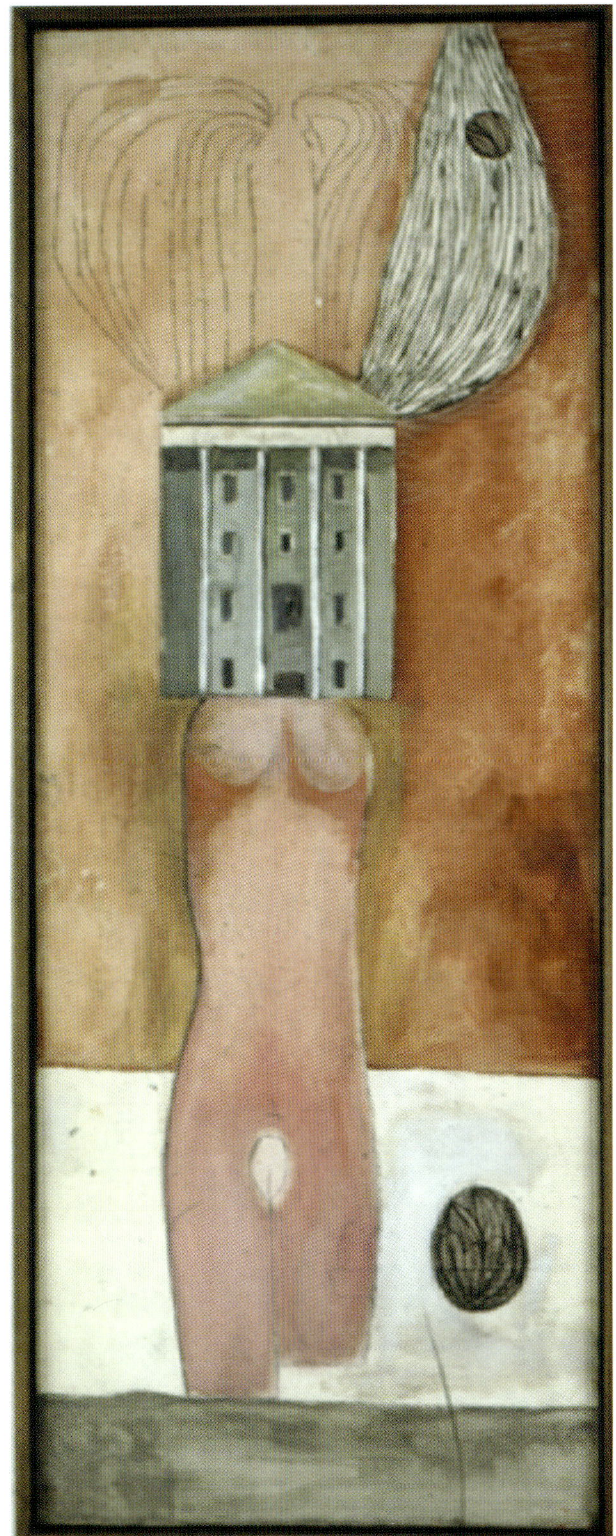

ouise Bourgeois, *Femme-Maison*, 1946-47.

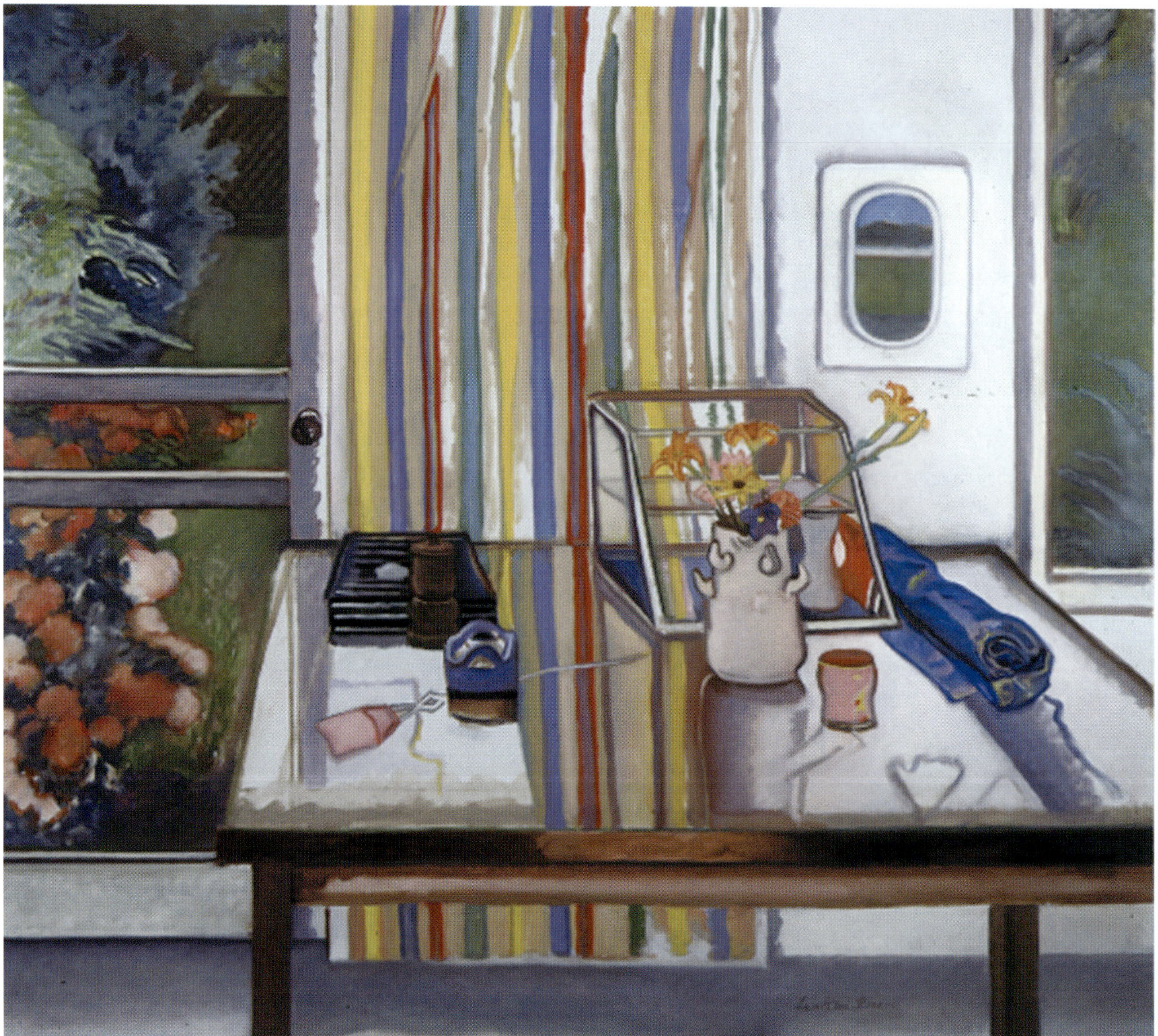

Leatrice Rose, *Summer Stripes*, ca. 1970.

As mysterious as a herd of animals galloping across a moonlit landscape is the interior of a silent room attached to its inescapable voyeur, the artist. Here the stage only appears to be domestic. Upon it a drama of exacting dimensions is waged between the eye and its object. The overexposure of what is considered elsewhere as impassioned painting with its inclusion of anguished figures who survive in under-delineated space, or that use of over-decorated space which attempts to survive without expression, has left these provocateurs unprepared for quiet rooms which impose their own reign of terror on the artist. Craftsmanship, sensibility, and above all, experience are at the gallows. Leatrice Rose, in her exhibition at the Armstrong Gallery, has brought a dazzling vocabulary of weapons to prove the impregnability of the silent room.

When she was a student at Washington Irving Art School, her teachers gave her an ultimatum: "You've just got to be a painter." Rose was in delighted agreement and after graduation she went on to study at Cooper Union. Recognizing the new directions that were being revealed to artists of her generation, she enrolled in Hans Hoffman's classes from whence she departed a confirmed Abstract Expressionist, or so it would seem from the painting she then produced and exhibited. Tom Hess, who kept watch over the spawning Hoffman students, recognized her as a gifted exponent of Abstract Expressionism.

In these youthful rapt days Rose believed that abstract painting (or the form which presented itself under the tutelage of Hoffman) was the only choice through which a breakthrough could be reached into a new concept of form. "Boundlessness" beckoned to her, as to so many of her generation. We see a restless progression of pictures until there begins a subtle entrance of what would be a seated figure, then another; they press their image into the expressionist technique. Perhaps the domestic tableaus of her life prompted her abstract, subjective painting into the real-life contours of children and the rooms in which a city life was enacted. A vision of the life-like was riding into abstraction. Slowly it arrived.

There appeared the seemingly meek portraits of a painter's daily motions: the palette, the easel, the window, the chair, the floor line, domestic alterations of landscape. Through abstraction she had arrived at what we choose to call realism (or so it appeared). If we study closely what would be the beginning of this realism, we discover that Rose is not an orthodox representationalist but is very close to Cubism in these realistic paintings. She presents us with ideas of forms, ideas of stationary objects which have an essentially Cubist sense of design that betrays her early, seasoned training. As Willem de Kooning remarked, "When I was a classical painter, that is when I was a Cubist . . . " Rose's realistic paintings are classical in that their underground is Cubist, the mind's eye of contemporary art.

This exhibition marks a progression from 1973 toward a more forceful declarative statement of her aims. That softness which preceded (the blurred edge, the hints, only hints always of the landscape as in time) has disappeared. Inside an earlier tenderness of line, there was often experienced a nudging, sheltered silence. The silence remains, but in back of it, bolstering it up, is a shout.

Like any gifted artist, Rose is a person who has what in opera is known as *temperament.* In the 1970s and before, she used muted colors: grays (she is a master of the use of that difficult Ingres color), soft yellows, fainter ochres. Exhibiting consistently from 1973 to 1985, and likely abetted by her teaching position at the Art Student's League, the coolness and detachment gradually have removed themselves. This exhibition is her strongest statement to date. It is a synthesis of the early and late. There is, as always, but now more consistently, a display of technique that is virtuoso. In *Summer Stripes* it would be an error to see the carefully positioned objects, the definitive stripes of the curtains, as an arrangement.

This painting is a study in ideas, an attempt to get behind the arrangement. She is willing both to abstract herself from the picture and to lean upon the personal stratagems arising from her awareness of the depth of painting. All these pictures are paintings about the art of painting.

Water Front is visually the most unproblematic and pleasing of the paintings. This picture has a quality of that sublimeness earlier associated with that "boundlessness" of abstraction. It is a complicated painting rendered easy, a view that doesn't brood, as if one took the mood out of Whistler's views of the lower Thames, the harshness out of the Hoboken waterfront, a way of turning the unnatural into nature.

The most startling picture is *Black Counter.* Here the artist judged her risks. The counter faces a painting of what appears to be a view of city wharves nearly eclipsed by an extraordinary Ryderesque sky. The counter is black; on it is a dark siphon bottle. Placed on a wooden stool which stands shortly below the counter is a vase holding feathery flowers; upon this stool is draped material with stripes. The lower left section of the painting is devoted to the puzzling arabesque of an iron stool. The bare bones of its iron seat would have charmed Max Ernst. Thus several paintings exist here within one painting. *Black Counter* astonishes me.

This is a daring work by an artist whose essential stance toward her paintings led us to believe she would never permit her pragmatism to be outweighed by the mystical. That she is matter-of-fact, dispossessed of any awe, her intensity leashed, surprises us, revealing a sensibility that is not altogether what it had seemed to be.

Today, Leatrice Rose, continuing as always to take matters into her own hands (the picture never runs away from her), may have decided quite objectively to permit her surprises to reveal themselves. There is more than a hint in this exhibition that having proved once again her control over her environment, she will let in strange airs and noises. In *Summer Stripes* we are permitted to look through a screened door upon a suspiciously lighted garden. Nature itself can become wickedly strange, Rose is saying to us. It may elude the grasp of dogmatism and lie beyond our personal projection of the real into the unknown of the surreal.

Observation, concentration, and candor are rarities at any time. In this exhibition Rose decided to wear her coat of many colors (projectile colors and those unabashedly hiding their subtleties), announcing more firmly than ever before their objectives, and leading us further into an unprotected, ambitious future.

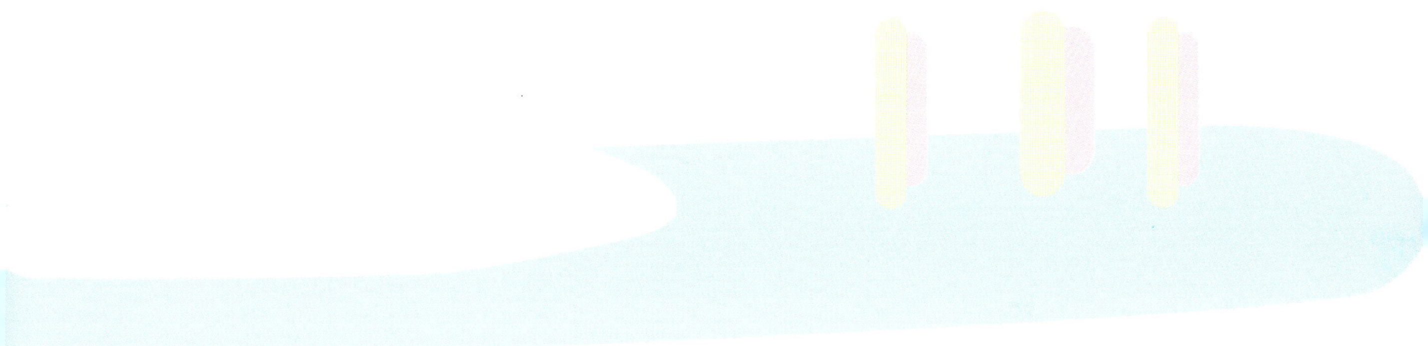

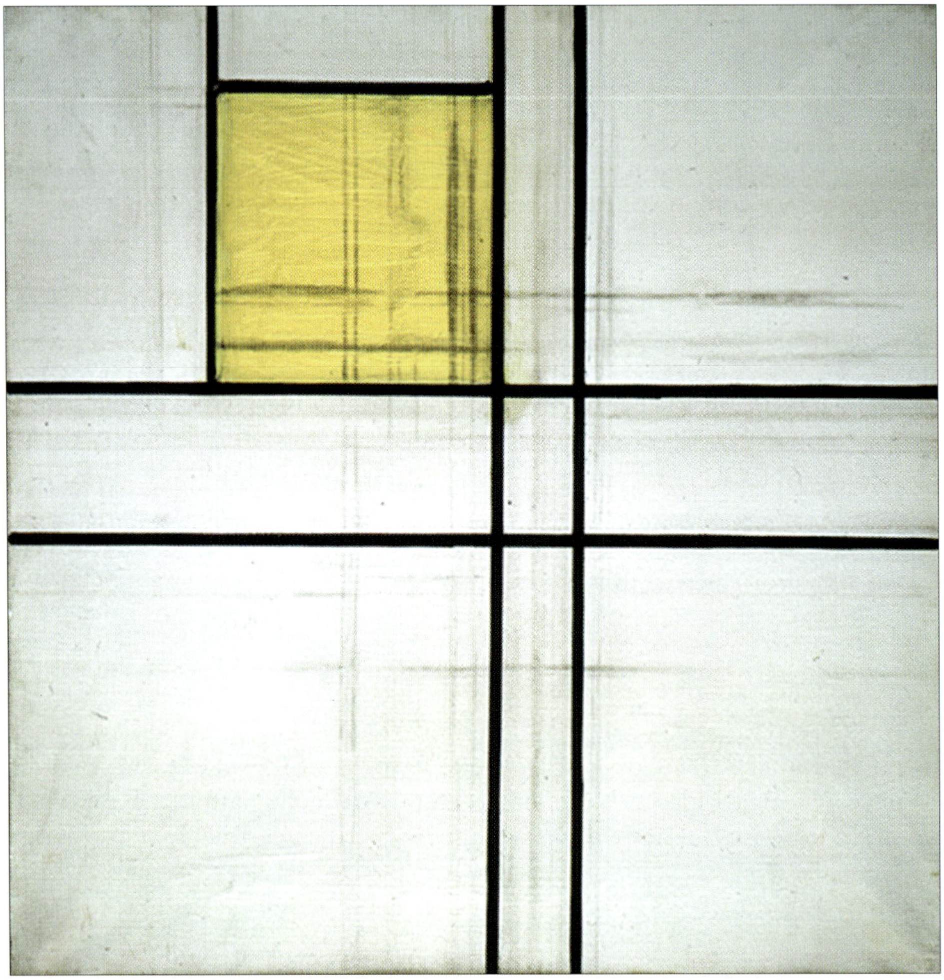

Piet Mondrian, *Composition with Yellow* (unfinished), 1934.

The beautiful, spatial Mondrian of 1922, *Composition with Blue, Black, Yellow and Red* was reproduced in the Art Section of *The New York Times* (January 7, 2000). We are grateful to the Harvard Museums who have acquired this masterpiece so pristine and fresh, sheltered in a private collection in Holland. The painting had never left Holland, even for a journey to another collection. Astoundingly it had never been displayed. We learn that "the painting had never been cleaned, restored or damaged, and even retains its original wood strip frame." The spirit of Mondrian, bruised in other paintings, somehow meddled with, impoverished as the "Studio of Mondrian" erected in the Museum of Modern Art, survives in this painting.

It is intact, even in a photograph, "the shiny black lines and fine brushwork, subtle gray tones and sharp primary colors." We see how Mondrian "carefully adjusted the lines and planes as they reached the edge of the canvas."

As they touch the edge of Modernity.

In the 1950's I left Los Angeles where I had lived with my Aunt and Uncle, attending high school and going to college, first at UCLA, later graduating from U.C. at Berkeley. I had lived in Los Angeles after I graduated, working at several jobs, but I was dissatisfied and friends suggested I go to New York.

A friend let me live in her apartment until her roommate returned which was very soon, I had begun to like living on Eighth Street in the dark apartment with few windows, but it was necessary that I leave. New Yorkers, however, looked after each other. The friend and her roommate did not wish to turn me out of the apartment. They suggested I call another friend who lived in a fifth floor walk-up, as New Yorkers called those apartments bare of conveniences such as elevators. Bathtubs stood on four legs in the kitchen. "Frieda" let me stay in her apartment, which was also just across the street from the Hans Hoffman School of modern painting.

Frieda Egger was from Austria, and she dedicated herself to her art and to a life of hardship, taking on small jobs when they were offered. The small amount I offered her helped out. As a consequence I did not complain when I was bitten by bedbugs. I learned about painters from her conversation, and about dedication, incidentally, stepping into the spilling-over bathtub, mopping up the water, washing my bites.

One day she suggested we go next door to another studio where an artist was working on a painting. I was not prepared for the cozy cottagey design of the apartment, the maple color of the furniture, the overstuffed chairs. I believed that artists should live like Frieda with bare walls and empty shelves and hard beds. The artist suggested we go into her studio. I was reluctant, believing the studio would be cozy with uninteresting drawings.

A painting, I was told it was by the artist, Mondrian, stood in the center. It would have been for him perhaps his "middle" period. Several years before *Broadway Boogie Woogie*, yet not the classic Mondrian of this earlier painting in *The New York Times*. Mondrian! The artist had been asked by the Museum of Modern Art to copy his painting.

There it stood in this tenement building, five stories up with snow on the fire escape. So large it took up most of the room. Shiny furniture from a department store in the next room.

The artist was unknown to me. His painting was unappreciated by me. I was afraid of the painting, of its emptiness. The carefully ruled, so I thought, spaces of color. The rigors, the hurdles of the painting, the sense of form from which it derived, the "emptiness," the knowledge and spatiality, were lost on me. The imperviousness of the painting was lost on me.

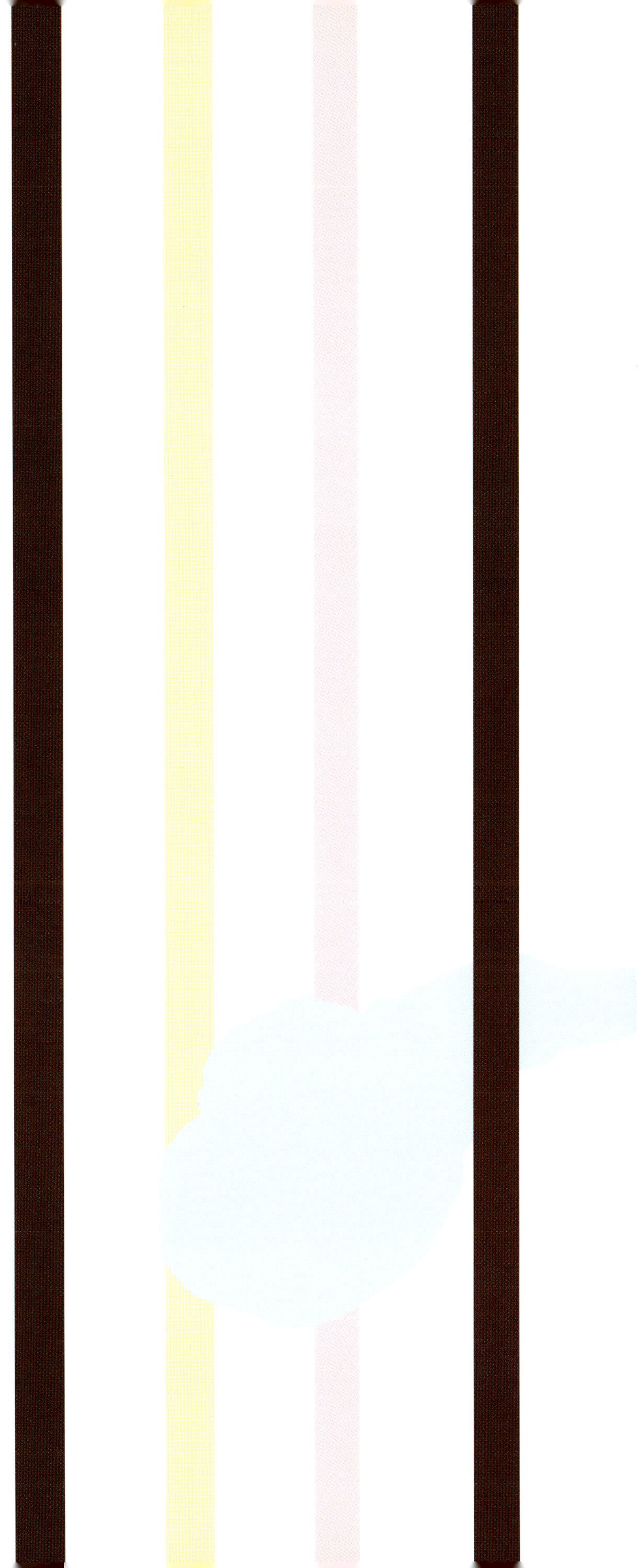

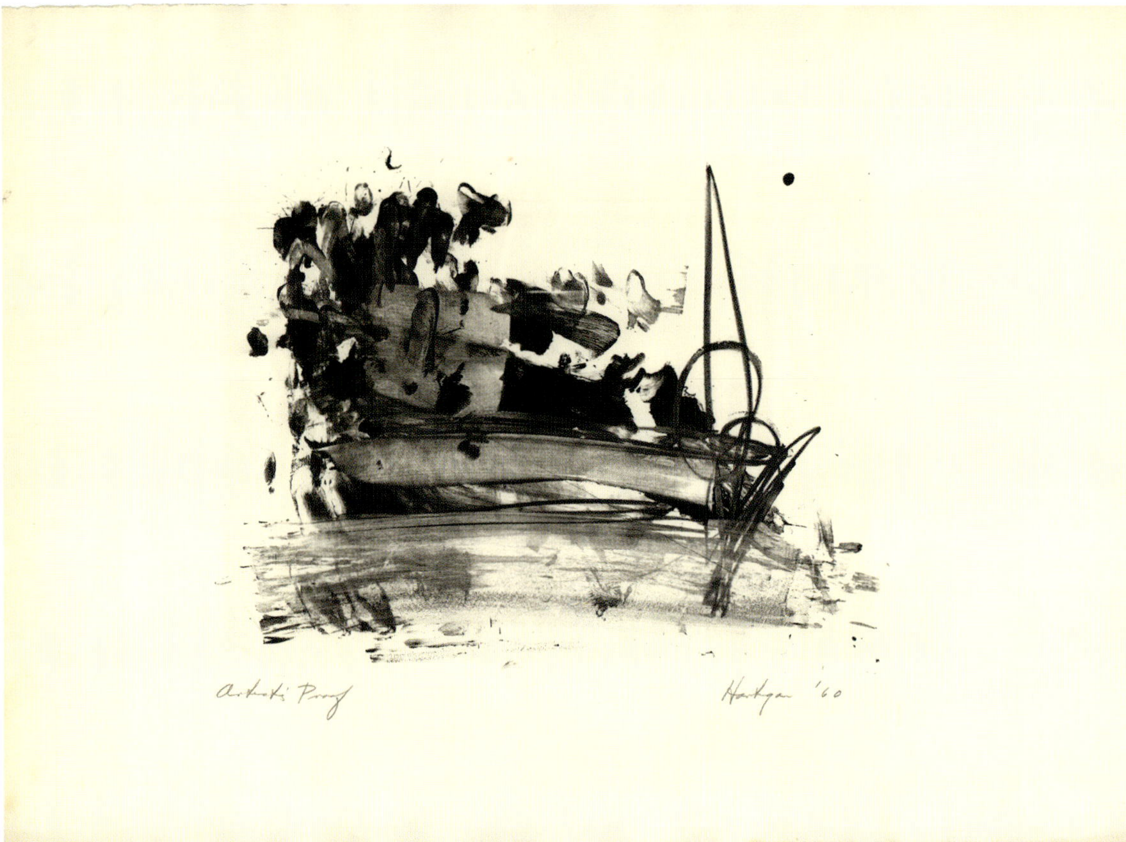

Grace Hartigan, *The Hero Leaves His Ship*, 1960.

THE HERO LEAVES HIS SHIP

I wonder if this new reality is going to destroy me.
There under the leaves a loaf
The brick wall on it someone has put bananas
The bricks have come lose under the weight,
What a precarious architecture these apartments,
As giants once in a garden. Dear roots
Your slivers repair my throat when anguish
commences to heat and glow.

From the water
A roar. The sea has its own strong wrist
The green turf is made of shells
it is new.

I am about to use my voice
Why am I afraid that salty wing
Flying over a real hearth will stop me?

Yesterday the yellow
Tokening clouds. I said 'no' to my burden,
The shrub planted on my shoulders. When snow
Falls or in rain, birds gather there
In the short evergreen. They repeat their disastrous
Beckoning songs as if the earth
Were rich and many warriors coming out of it,
As if the calm was blue, one sky over
A shore and the tide welcoming a fleet
Bronzed and strong as breakers,

Their limbs in this light
Fused of sand and wave are lifted once
Then sunk under aquamarine, the phosphorous.

Afterwards the soundless bay,
Gulls fly over it. The dark is mixed
With wings. I ask if that house is real,
If geese drink at the pond, if the goatherd takes
To the mountain, if the couple love and sup,

I cross the elemental stations
from windy field to still close. Good night I go to my bed.
This roof will hold me. Outside the gods survive.

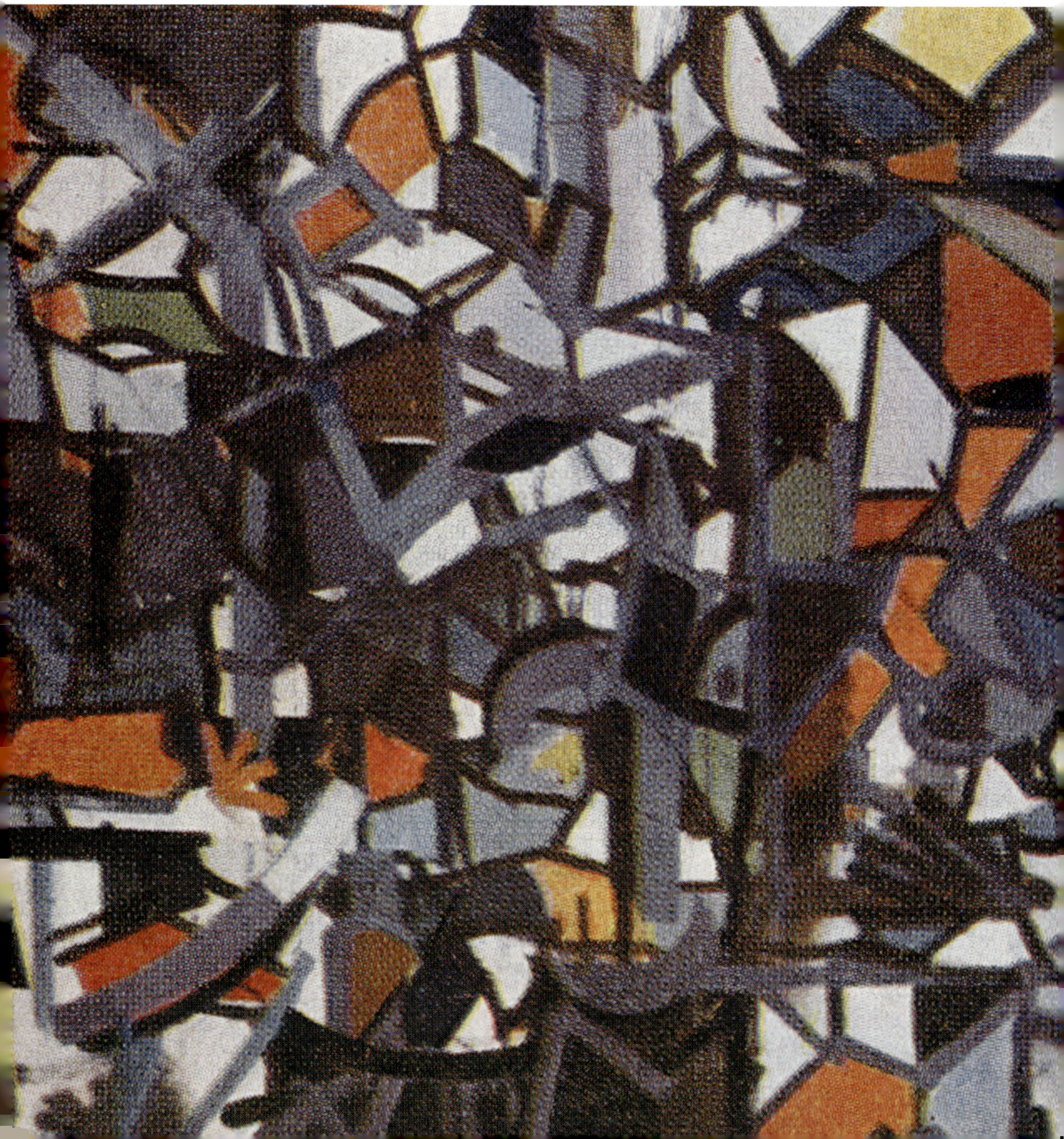

In today's academy Robert Goodnough is an anomaly. He is not an Abstract Expressionist, nor is he a non-Objective painter. He belongs to no group, indeed he appears to have chosen few personal contacts within the New York School. He exchanges his ideas privately with himself, and the rest is silence. The painting is non-verbal. It contains an inner monologue. His painting expresses none of the immediacy of a secret suddenly understood and given quick life on the canvas that we are accustomed to experiencing from the Abstract Expressionists. Behind his darkened vertical lines or white lines exercising in a geometry of space, there usually stands a figure. It can be *The Mediator* or *The Centaur* or *Calamity Jane*. The figure is waiting in controlled inactivity to announce the meaning of the painting. A conflict of tension has taken place between the abstract foreground and the flattened shapes merged into small and large area of color and the image.

Unlike the Cubists for whom painting was a destruction of image into idea, Goodnough believes in a coexistence of separates. He has said, "I believe painting is a sum of parts, each independently important in creating a totality."

He began his picture geometrically with a structure of lines, mostly in grays. Squareness appeared and began to disappear (cubes are squared). Then he outlined shapes independent of the original structure. Then he began the breakdown of the cube; he thinks of "them" as flat areas. Now commences the battle between what he knows of traditional painting, i.e., Picasso, Matisse, Mondrian, and his own talent.

At this point when what can be called pure abstraction has been reached, Goodnough breaks off. He defines his own horizon. White chalk separates areas, the geometry breaks up, expands, the movement which has been located almost fiercely in the center turns outward: we are no longer in a regulated world of space defined by cubes and angles, we are pushed vigorously into the unknown.

Again he breaks off. His own horizons have been defined by the human figure and the idiosyncrasies of its personality. So far he has showed us the brilliancy of Art pure, now —because he is an abstractionist, who also believes in the humanist value of painting— he permits the figure to lay its just claims on his picture. He urges the unknown head, or coaxes inert shapes—all the time the artist was solving spatial problems, they had been serenely resting with perhaps a tail of a horse or a helmet of a warrior giving a clue to the immediacy of a foreign identity—to force their way into the open space of the painting. Goodnough proposes for us to examine, not only the surface, not only its identification with painting, but the fragment of an identity unabsorbed by the painting.

And what has the artist to say about this figure. "The figure is a symbol." The figure exists to clarify. What he has been doing with those strong black and white outlines, those brief entrances of color, is to bring clarity into his picture. He has been avoiding a blur or use of color that is merely mellifluous. He has made "edges" that will not become lost.

There is no disappearing. He wants us to see everything. As he remarked, "After Mondrian we don't see trees, we see wires." In this manner he has excused himself from action painting. How? By his very literalness, by his decision to tell "all" in a painting. Not the mysterious ALL, but all he knows about that particular painting engaging him. There are no empty areas, no shapes without a purpose. Collage intrigues him with its sense of order and arrangement. Collage is not a "thinking-out process" prior to the painting. Collage is not a means to an end. Within the shorter scope of collage, the distinctiveness toward which he works can appear much more rapidly, not as exercise, but as completed statement. A Goodnough collage may present more rapidly and more easily the image of the whole in his work. One can grasp the collage more readily. In a sense, the collage precedes the painting. All those collaged bits of painted canvas, how exactly they are placed, how they avoid the cliché, how pure they are eliminating so much that is unnecessary.

One never spoke of Goodnough as a "colorist." Up until now color has been subordinate. As a draughtsman we speak of him, a superior one, but he always draws. He draws in the air, before the first outline of the painting. As a student he was dedicated to drawing. However, one was never struck by the poverty of those canvas spaces; they were not empty. They were filled with thought, not color. Lately he has demonstrated what can be done by preparing for the natural attack of red, blue, yellow, without permitting a riot of color. The center of the painting bears the force; there his reds remain clear, blues send off light. Then as we divert our eyes from this central tension, we discover we are entering into deeper, more twilight colors of gray, as the painting finds its momentum, moving outward. We recognize this zoning and this modulation as both careful and modest. His colors remove the element of surprise. They have been dictated by the painting, itself, not the eye alone, or the heart, or even the willful memory of a landscape. The separate demands of each area of the painting that have laid its claim on him.

To find the picture, the animus, both physical and metaphysical. To be directed and to direct. To clarify and to intensify; to be absorbed and yet free. To allow thought to enter passion, as silence interrupts movement, these are at the urgencies of a Goodnough painting.

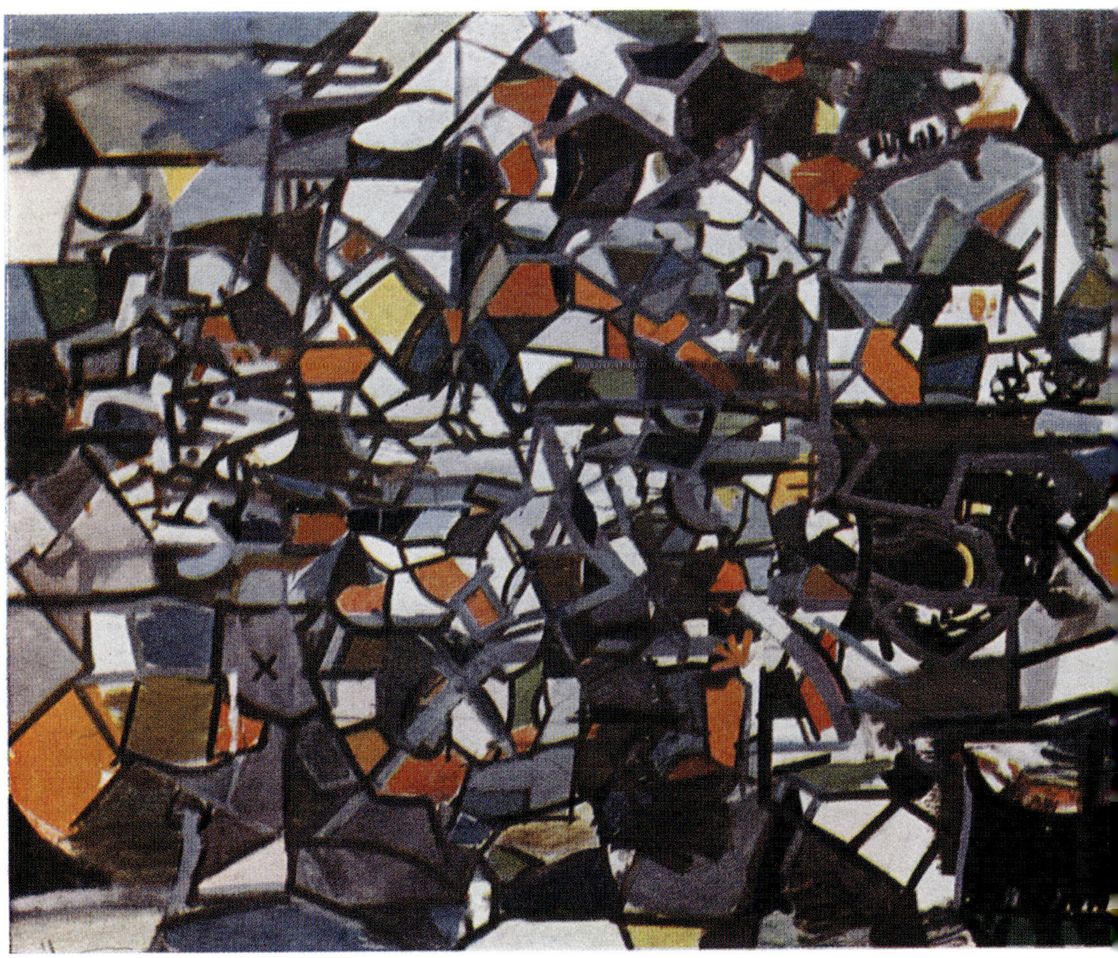

Robert Goodnough, *The Centaur*, 1959.

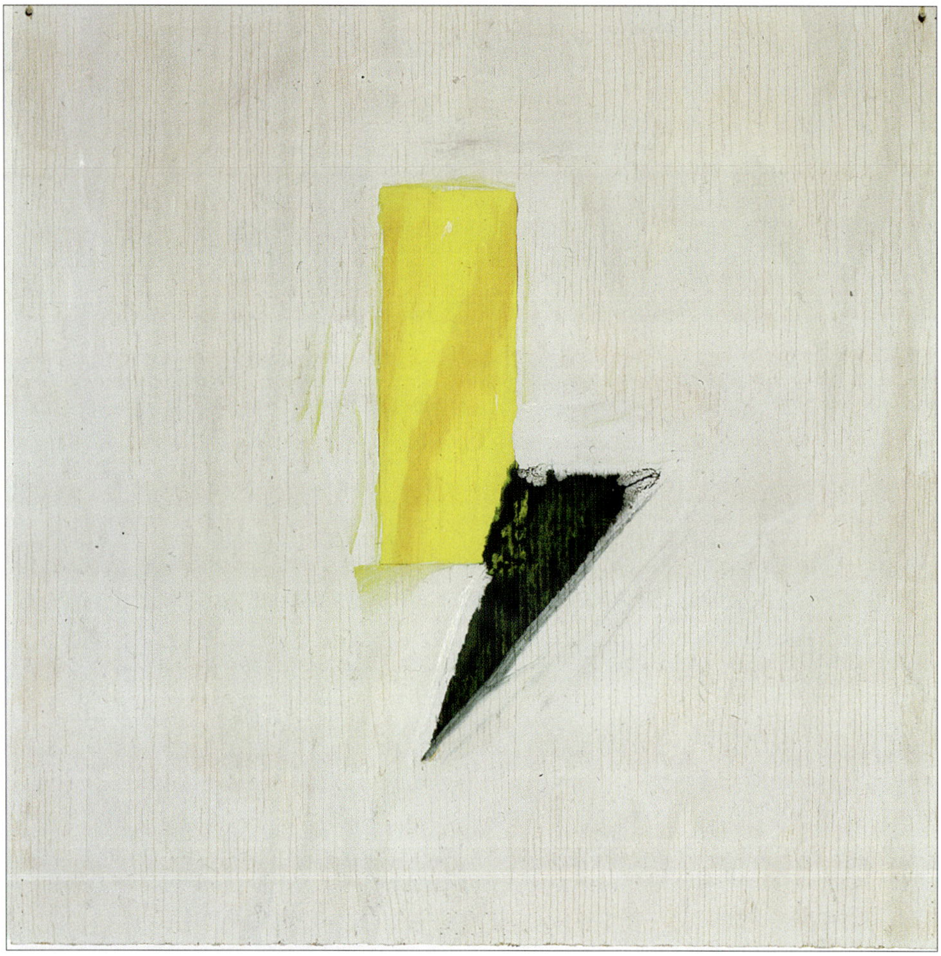

Richard Tuttle, *Overlap, A3*, 2000.

The Color Green in the Art Work of Richard Tuttle

GREEN IS A NOTORIOUSLY DIFFICULT COLOR IS THE SUPERSTITION. It is a serious color, slightly morose, somewhat intellectual. It is often found among the grays of countryside. It refuses to meddle with charm. Often green seems preoccupied, thoughtful. Green is not the color of heaven. It has a myriad of tasks to perform. Green must take up the burden of other colors on a page or canvas grown heavy with labor. Avoiding purple it sidles up to blue, knowing in the regime of color that blue is thoughtful. Indoors, unless under the panoply of heaven, an aristocratic color, even gay in the eighteenth century. Green has trouble with the heavens, being practical.

Green is willing to labor, and often works into the night when other colors dim their lights.

When Richard Tuttle is painting, I examine the surface he works on to see if it is a hilly terrain, requiring the labor of green to maintain the spirit of the artist, to declare it is in on earth he labors. Green often comes to the aid of the artist in a difficult situation, when the canvas refuses to speak.

A refusal now causes Tuttle to summon green. The artist is patient, he does not prod or command his color he waits patiently, he searches, almost superstitiously for the right place for color to place its spirit upon the surface the artist prepared. The artist is friendly to green, he treats green conversationally, and often charms the green that appears on his brush. Green can hold a picture together; it has the power of adhesion.

The artist now provides space for the green comforter of the emotions, reminder of the green provisions.

Courbet, who moved amid a dry country landscape respected this color and even hid it in the bedclothes of courtesans. On the hunting caps of female riders his green is triumphant.

Manet chose to spread in a green wood a picnic with green resources. Delacroix used the color on his ceilings; green shaded the parks he walked in.

Picasso, in search of invention hid the green nature of his constructions.

Each artist embarks on a personal research, and Tuttle may expect an introspective refreshment from green. And then, again, as if he seized a water sprinkler to hint at rinsed green, so will this tone almost jokingly spread itself among other colors, noisetone from a hunting horn when the new color is overtaken. He created intimacy he wants to exist among the primary colors elevating themselves when low-spirited.

Tuttle is consistent in his choice of subject. He likes to surprise the viewer. The surprise is a subsidiary of his technique. We can rely on the setting in which a painting is poised to surprise us. This word surprise may also be a surprise to the artist. Even when clues have been memorized from past artwork. This is the most gala surprise.

The artist gives us an assurance that memory never ceases to flow from the unconscious, an attitude natural to this artist. He cannot abandon the memory of color. If he makes the decision to feature certain colors, the entire spectrum may be linked to the process of recall before the choice is made. Or so it can appear to the viewer, overwhelmed by the glow. If a slice of green rests on yellow, that slice has a territorial claim.

Color initiates form. Part of an instinctive formula in the background of Richard Tuttle it never exits. A loss of one of the starry patterns, perhaps, but not dispossessed. Color remains this artist's alphabet.

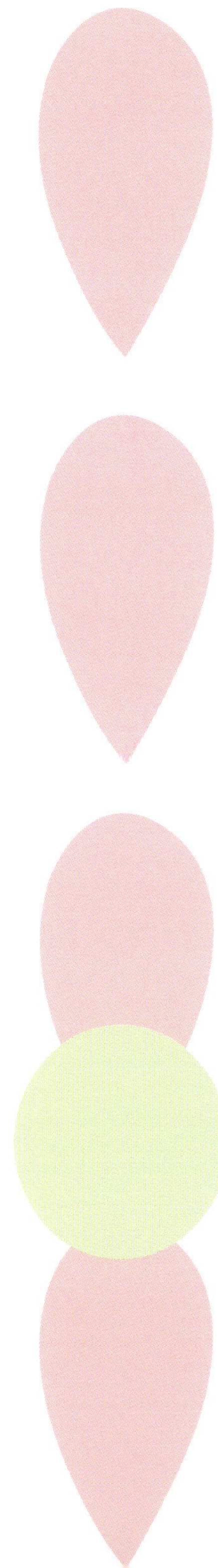

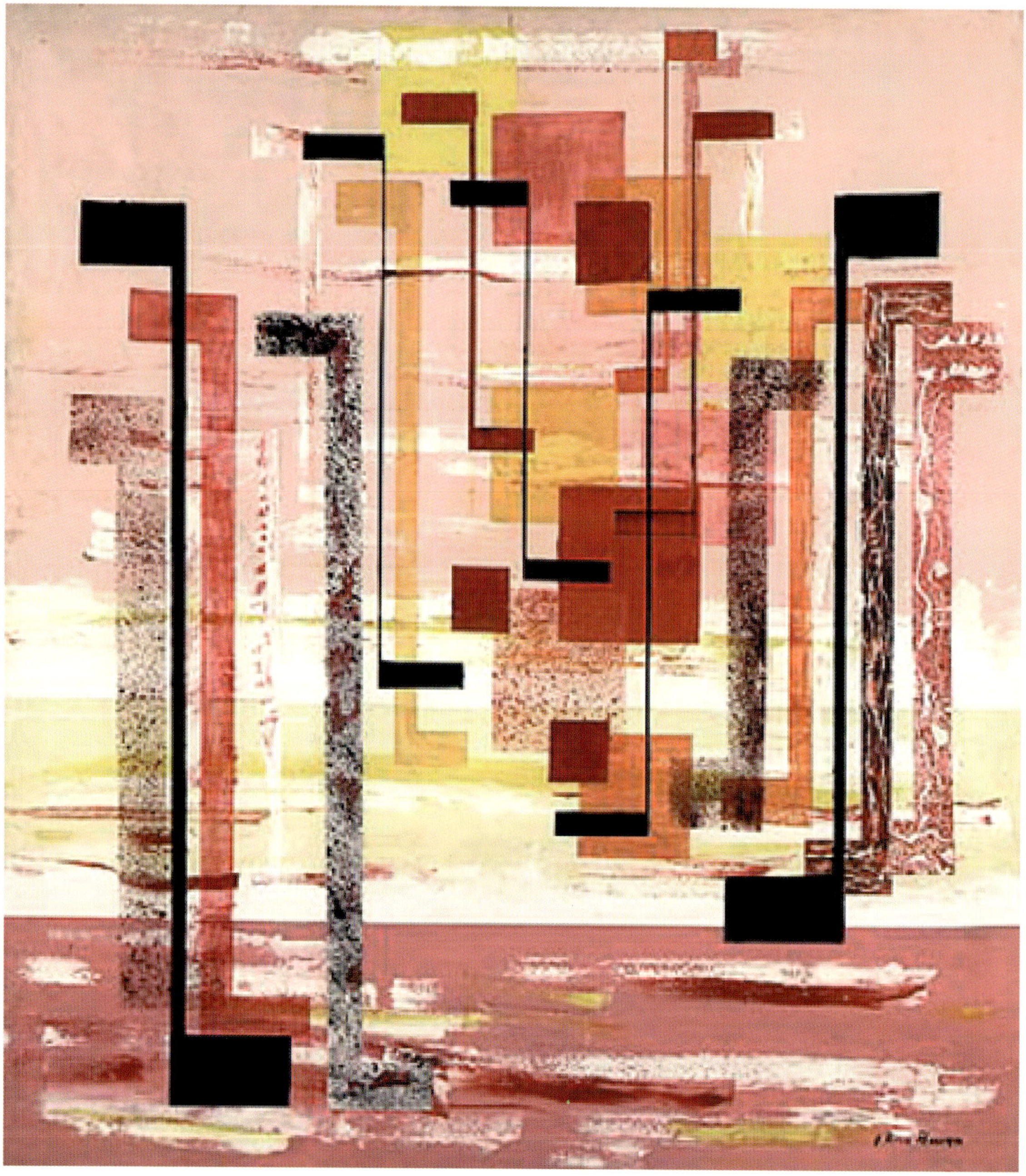

I. Rice Pereira, *Heart of Flame*, c. 1945.

The Shadow of Surrealism

I grew up under the shadow of Surrealism. In that creative atmosphere of magical rites there was no recognized separation between the arts. Those of us who shared this atmosphere brightened by Apollinaire, Eluard, Valéry and the old master Mallarmé, considered ourselves part of a hemisphere where all the arts evolved around one another, a central plaza with roads which led from the palette to quill to clef. One could never again look at a locked kingdom. Poetry extended vertically, as well as horizontally, never did it lie motionless within a linear structure. Assisting in this poetic mobility would be an associative art within whose eye the poet might gaze for reassurance and for a glowing impersonal empathy.

We have read of the relation of Gertrude Stein to Picasso. She saw her own work and Cubist painting as engaged in a similar struggle. She even went so far as to write Cubist portraits. What she was actually seeking was an escape from literature, or from the "literary," and she saw and envied the freedom shared by Picasso, Braque and Gris in their breakthrough from formalism to Cubism. Painters were the revolutionaries to whom writers turned their desire to break from the solemnity of the judicious rules of their craft.

This need to go on a rampage was felt by poets during the explosive era of Abstract Expressionism. We ended by admiring not only the work of painters with its "action," which meant breaking the rules, acting upon the canvas the otherwise concealed emotional and environmental state of the painter; we became envious of the activity of their personal lives.

This may appear to be a frivolous remark, but it contains a metaphor in which the natural gravity of life is replaced by the gratification of secret desires. Art as reflection became more instantaneous, willful, enthusiastic, freed by action. Painters naturally gravitated toward expensive cars, lofts and chateaux, while poets take buses, settle in dim rooms (with the exception of Rilke) and until the event of the word processor satisfied themselves with modestly turned print. Money rolls into the pockets of painters with a frequency that stuns the poet. Just as the extravagance of a painter is admired so is his ability to leap the boundaries of experiment or assume the labors of a chauvinist past. Some of us did desire to sit under the same umbrella as Picasso, even share his villa at Mougins. The physical extravagance of paint, of enormous canvases can cause a nurturing envy in the poet that prods his greatest possession, the imagination, into an expansion of its borders.

As an art critic, who happened to be a poet, I was exposed to the temperament of the explosion of Abstract Expressionism. My personal relationships with its painters certainly influenced the way I saw both nature and image. It was a poet, Frank O'Hara, who in a poem described the process of Abstract Expressionism far more intuitively than any critic or art historian.

Lunch at Helen Frankenthaler's

I wake up
                    what was I dreaming about?
"Mountains & Sea"   a cloud
a hand over the cloud.   Is it China
that arranges itself thus?
                              Early China
before envelopes?

                      There is a figure in the landscape
no not at all   the sea
on which an old man embarks in a canoe,
what is this? a picnic in the canoe?
It isn't a man in that boat   the kimono
is wrapped,   how does one say   it is a woman!
It's Helen!   her face with its arbor of thunder
and laurel starts to drift over the mountain

                      Helen!
we're having lunch!
                      Return
in your snow boots,
                          here's the thermos
I've poured out so many words, and the sandwiches
prepared with watercress.   Blissful
sentences begin with "Do you remember . . ."
and "After August,"   and "I saw you in a red cloak."

                      Helen!
don't jump into that pillar of statues!

                      without you there is no lunch.

The Nude

Studios are stations of reminiscence
in the nimble wind they are shadows

The artist attaches himself to the shadow
he attempts to revive it after the wind ceases,

This mixture of dark and light
is mysterious and adds depth

To the position of his model
who rephrases the shadow.

She reminds him of attitudes
beyond the mere appraisal of subject,

A peace without clothes
with its bestowal of light and volume

Where nudism is born.

The behavior of the landscape of nudism
varies as mirrors reflect

Curves, syllables of grace,
drops of water or trees elastic,

A native body beneath its plumes.

Is a weight become effervescent
when attacked by knowledge

Of shells and other remainders
of sexual consciousness tossed from sand,

They live in a contradiction of time.

The narcissism of the artist escapes into a body
that defines his emotions,

An interior where his own contour is less misty.

The figure is a nominal reminder that existence
is not pantomime as relieved by the artist,

The body of the model, the lift of her torso
the extension of limbs, fold of skin

Express reality beyond tenure of the brush,
shell or escapist sail,

A severe distance is established between her realism
and his anxious attempt to define it.

The painter desires the image he has selected
to be clothed in the absolute silk of his touch,

Lonely himself he has admired the glance
of kimonos, mirrors, fans and bestowed them on her

Who for many minutes of this day
borrows from art to cover her nudity.

The artist chose these objects to enrich space
around his model's hair or even her breathing

Which you notice as it shifts the atmosphere
in which you keep watch with a calm become necessary,

You are the viewer and without you
the picture cannot exist, the model shall cease to breathe.

The artist will sorrow even as darkness replaces
his brilliance of color.

The viewer inherits this nude
as a reminder of his own weightlessness

In a natural world
made winsome, or tense or aggravated

By the requests of an unclad body
with its announcement of dimension and clarity.

The need of the artist to draw the body
is like the love for three oranges,

He searches the world to find those spheres
that will confine the fluid nude,

There is with him a desire elemental
in its urgency to savor the skin of the body

The hues of geranium before they exit
his allotment of reality.

As the swan entered Leda
so the actual timing of an artist's abrupt gesture

Is supernatural despite interferences
of local ornamental mundaneity,

The supernatural contacts ecstasy hidden
in a guise of nudism.

The artist borrows mannerisms and technique,
he is free to copy, the other world is ambitionless.

An aura once restless now subsists
through residual favors on reverence,

Eve stands by her cypress,
a quiet nude studied by Cranach,

The solid body is led through crocuses.

You are with an artist who notices everything
which concerns color and shape.

In the restaurant the artist says a blouse
you are wearing goes with the decor.

The blouse is a watery blue like somewhere
off the coast of Greece, like these walls

The colors you wear tumble into mild earth tones
again like a country, nothing literary

Where the rough body reaches out
a wave rushes over the sand denuding it

You share the classical nude landscape of sand.

At times a silence overcomes the artist,
a fog at the base of columns,

He explains he is thinking of the body

Its behavior is strange, hiding behind leaves
he can never trap or bribe it.

So deep is the body's memory of self.

Each day there is a different voice,
today while wearing no clothes

It spoke of the essentials of life which were evident,
but the body took an invisible position,

It is arguable whether he shall ever see the face,
her back was turned from him like a goddess

She was either admiring herself or bathing.

Morning traverses her breasts
where she sits under the window of white curtains,

Trees are outside, their branches fix the sky,
she is thinking of nudism,

He draws an odalisque,
it is love they are asking for.

She looks at a canvas,
nature covets it,

Where a fever blots the muslin
clouds start to rise.

There is no figure.

This is landscape,
portrait of nude melancholy

Or its glow which is austere,
she asks, where am I?

He has not drawn her,
the sheen of her body only survives.

She turns herself into a star
above the unattended foliage,

He views her as she glistens,
silver enters the picture.

He confides,
"Each day I define myself."

He notices a coarseness of flesh,
he thickens his paint,

"It is a glimpse into the future,
fields light up," she sighs.

To replenish the sallow on her throat
he adds sunset tint

She reaches for ombre, noir
"It is the narrowness of time."

Respectful moonlight inhabits them.

On a Painting by Haydn Stubbing

Where is the sky?
Here.
And the unknowingness
Of shadows?
There.

Bracken, furze, field,
The picture bending over
To describe itself
As who, not always a
There.

The leaf treads, skies
Throng into themselves;
Water is not far off,
A blessing made of the music
Of turf.

Skimmed as frost
Forms a place on the inner
Scale, becomes easier
When it is learned
Winter begins.

The harvest
Is there in the branches
And whatever says,
"My goodness, I've thunder
In my boughs."

That person who framed
The fair weather clouds
Bestowed wisdom
To the tips of leaves,
Saying, “a chance of showers.”
While you paint
The picture's skin.

So it will be robust,
Yet ambiguous like autumn
Whose thoughts tangling
With spectrum
Never recognize
Their green pronouncing,

Pampered as visionary wind
Deciding whatever burden
It will tote away
Into that space
The picture elects
To purify.

The Poetess
[*after* Miró]

A dollop is dolloping
her a scoop is pursuing
flee vain ignots Ho
coriander darks thimble blues
red okays adorn her
buzz green circles in flight
or submergence? Giddy
mishaps of blackness make
stinging clouds what!
a fraught climate
what natural c/o abnormal
loquaciousness the
Poetess riddled
her aserisk is there
genial! as space

Homage

"A New Era of the Plastic Arts had Begun."
Frederick Kiesler*

The world
is going upstairs
and some people
of whom Kiesler
doesn't approve
are sitting in the basement.

Galaxies Galaxies

You are our last jewel,
and we preserved you
in our ateliers.

A morning
was one day to open
over the roof tops,

and we see dawn
as a galaxy,

having in sleep
experienced original dreams,
now become an environment.

We climb into the night suit,
no longer traditional,
or isolated, the future
in another scale,

Galaxy! Galaxies!
entering from the moon.

* Frederick Kiesler melded large, slender "balls" of interwoven metal, he called "Galaxies." They were the first "Mobiles." They may have originated in his architectural drawings. Kiesler designed the Peggy Guggenheim Gallery in New York where Pollock and a "galaxy" of new painters first showed.

The Lost Speech

Archaeology
With a lift of brown and occupation,
Archaeology

on layers of limestone that protects a lost speech in the thick
wood plundered.
A search for past occupational diversions.

Let history commandeer your tongue at this
elevation.

It is nothing to grow wings. To be La Favorita.

A girl wearing satin and wings makes a speech,
Then ventured outside, a cloak thrown over her shoulders.

The Macedonians know how to plunder, to thieve, yet they
lifted

La Favorita from that overturned ship,
And sent her back to the Lycians.

NOTES and CITATIONS

ARTnews

Stephen Etnier, December 1952, pg. 43.
Childe Hassam, December 1952, pg. 43.
Beerbohm and Robinson, January 1953, pg. 46.
Theodore Stamos, January 1953, pg. 47.
Richard Stankiewicz, January 1953, pgs. 50 & 64.
Ludwig Bemelmans, January 1953, pg. 48.
John Wilde, January 1953, pg. 50.
Edward John Stevens Jr., February 1953, pg 72.
Master Drawings, March 1953, pg. 36.
Ludwig Wolpert, Summer 1953, pg. 64.
Norwegian Serigraphs, Summer 1953, pgs. 65-66.
Gustav Wolf, November 1953, pgs. 60-61.
New York Society of Women Artists, December 1953, pg. 36.
Alfonso Ossorio, January 1954, pg. 68.
Richard Lindner, February 1954, pg. 44.
Enrico Donati, February 1954, pg. 44.
Moura Chabor, February 1954, pg. 60.
Cuno Amiet, March 1954, pgs. 40-41.
Louise Nevelson, May 1954, pg. 43.
Alfred Leslie, May 1954, pg. 43.
Younger American and European Painters, June 1954, pg. 56.
Nachum Gutman, June 1954, pgs. 71-72.

ESSAYS and COLLABORATIONS

Jean Arp, presented at Poet's House, New York. (Date unavailable.)
Joan and Ken and Thinking, Barbara Guest & Joe Brainard, ink on paper, 14 by 8", *C Comics 1*, 1964, exhibited University Art Museum, University of California, Berkeley, April, 2001.
June Felter, *Art in America*, March, 1991.
Helen Frankenthaler, The Moment and The Distance. (Date unavailable.)
Honey or Wine?, Barbara Guest & Mary Abbott, 1971, National Gallery of Art, Washington, D.C.
Louise Bourgeois, "Why Has Louise Bourgeois Finally Become the Artist of the Moment," *Denver Quarterly*, 28, no. 1 (1993) 72-76.
Leatrice Rose, *Arts Magazine*, 1985.
Piet Mondrian, 2000.
"Robert Goodnough," in *School of New York: Some Younger Artists*, edited by B.H. Friedman, New York: Grove Press, 1959.
Richard Tuttle, 2000.
The Shadow of Surrealism, originally presented in the Kouros Gallery, New York, 1986.

POETRY

"Egypt" from *Moscow Mansions,* a Richard Seaver book. New York: Viking Press, 1973.

"The Hero Leaves His Ship," from *POEMS. The Location of Things. Archaics. The Open Skies.* New York: Doubleday and Company, Inc., 1962.

"Lunch at Helen Frankenthaler's." (Date unavailable.)

"The Nude," from Warren Brandt, New York: Art Editions, 1989; reprinted in *Fair Realism.* Los Angeles: Sun & Moon, 1989.

"On a Painting by Haydn Stubbing," previously unpublished.

"The Poetess," from *Moscow Mansions,* a Richard Seaver book. New York: Viking Press, 1973.

"Homage," 1964.

"The Lost Speech," 1964, reprinted in *Women's Studies*, 2001, Vol. 30, and in *Miniatures*, Wesleyan, CT: Wesleyan University Press, 2002.

Dürer in the Window was composed in
Americana, Baurer Bodoni, Caslon,
Courier, Janson, Scotch, Time,
Wilke and Zurick.
Printed in Hong Kong
through Global Interprint
on Shinho 128 gsm matte art paper.